UNIVERSITY OF NORTH CAROLINA AT CHAPEL HILL
DEPARTMENT OF ROMANCE LANGUAGES

NORTH CAROLINA STUDIES
IN THE ROMANCE LANGUAGES AND LITERATURES

Founder: URBAN TIGNER HOLMES
Editor: MARÍA A. SALGADO

Distributed by:

UNIVERSITY OF NORTH CAROLINA PRESS

CHAPEL HILL
North Carolina 27515-2288
U.S.A.

NORTH CAROLINA STUDIES IN THE
ROMANCE LANGUAGES AND LITERATURES
Number 242

JORGE LUIS BORGES
AND HIS PREDECESSORS

JORGE LUIS BORGES AND HIS PREDECESSORS

or

Notes Towards a Materialist History of Linguistic Idealism

BY

MALCOLM K. READ

CHAPEL HILL

NORTH CAROLINA STUDIES IN THE ROMANCE
LANGUAGES AND LITERATURES

U.N.C. DEPARTMENT OF ROMANCE LANGUAGES

1993

Library of Congress Cataloging-in-Publication Data

Read, Malcolm K. (Malcolm Kevin), 1945-
  Jorge Luis Borges and his predecessors, or, Notes towards a materialist history of linguistic idealism / Malcolm K. Read.
    p. – cm. – (North Carolina Studies in the Romance Languages & Literatures; 242).
    Includes bibliographical references.
    ISBN 0-8078-9246-7 (pbk).
    1. Borges, Jorge Luis, 1899- – Philosophy. 2 Criticism. 3. Argentina – Intellectual life – 19th century. 4. Argentina – Intellectual life – 20th century. I. Title. II. Title: Notes towards a materialist history of linguistic idealism. III. Series.

PQ7797.B635Z85 1993   92-80589
868 – dc20   CIP

© 1993. Department of Romance Languages. The University of North Carolina at Chapel Hill.

ISBN 0-8078-9246-7

DEPÓSITO LEGAL: V. 1.783 - 1993   I.S.B.N. 84-599-3317-2

ARTES GRÁFICAS SOLER, S. A. - LA OLIVERETA, 28 - 46018 VALENCIA - 1993

For Jesse, Garit and Conrad

"The bourgeois viewpoint has never advanced beyond [the] antithesis between itself and [the] romantic viewpoint, and therefore the latter will accompany it as legitimate antithesis up to its blessed end."

Karl Marx

"So last romanticism comes into existence when it becomes fully realized that the grandiose claim of first romanticism, that the poetic imagination is the most significant thing the world has ever known, crashes on the rocks of skepticism *and yet survives.* When the much-wished for drowning and wondrous sea change do not come, what is left is the desire of the first romantic trapped within the impotent body of despairing, ironic man."

Frank Lentricchia

PREFACE

A Marxist structuralism that sees the subject as merely the "effect of system," entrapped by a dominant ideology, poses serious problems for those of us who, independently of any bourgeois notion of individual freedom, cherish that extraordinary emphasis on human creativity and self-creation which characterizes Marxism in its classic forms. How do we know that we do not know? What is involved in the struggle for human objectivity?

It scarcely seems necessary to justify the urgency with which I address such problems, or indeed to defend myself against charges of personal bias in their (attempted) resolution. In the last instance we are all bound to speak from the perspective of our direct involvement. For my own part, I confess to the wish to settle accounts with a tradition of British Hispanism in which I was nurtured, and which I have come to regard as intellectually narrow and suffocating.

In a sense, of course, one arrives too late upon the scene of disaster: the Academy has already been invaded by a political reality long deemed irrelevant to "practical criticism," whose insistence on the autotelic nature of the literary work effectively neutralized any attempt to locate it within an historical context. The goddess of Fortune is fickle indeed: it is now literary scholarship that must fend off charges of irrelevance. Perforce, it has been found wanting. The promotion of "background courses" on "Culture and Civilization" to foreground status has merely served to expose radical inadequacies, stemming from the virtual absence within British Hispanism of anything that could lay claim to being a serious tradition of cultural, sociological analysis.

To whom, or to what, do we ascribe our manifest shortcomings? What seems most remarkable, with the advantage of hindsight, is the capacity of the Academy to repress differences within society, and concomitantly to defuse the liberation of one's own discourse. The pressure to conform was enormous – how else was one to get on? – and, to a degree, irresistible. But it is not merely our vulnerability that is at issue: we also need to scrutinize our capacity for corruptibility. Personally, I find it depressing in retrospect to chart the cumulative effect of daily compromises, the process of seduction within the ideological practice of a critical establishment that contributed directly, if not crucially, to the maintenance and reproduction of capitalist social relations. Gradually, almost without my realizing it, the traditional socialism, which at one time formed part of the air I breathed, became a dull recollection, a mild irritant, the source of some vague, unassuaged sense of guilt.

Was it luck that took me to Jamaica in 1987 as visiting professor? Traumatic as the experience was, such an idea seems almost unthinkable. Yet it remains surely one of life's greatest ironies that we learn most from its bitterest lessons. I have always known what any working-class boy who seeks to "better himself" soon discovers to his cost, that University campuses are surrounded by high walls and barbed-wire fences, but the palpable, literal reality that I encountered in Jamaica was far more imposing than my previous experience of the strictly metaphorical barriers to higher education. I had always known that the tragedies of life, far from being imponderable, insoluble, and existential, as *calderonistas* assured us, concern the everyday, social realities of ordinary men and women, and cry out for political solution. But alas it took the blistering confrontation with Third World poverty to make me remember the milder deprivation I had known but chosen to forget. This book was written to preserve that remembrance, and thus to contribute, in no matter how small a way, to an understanding, and therefore to the supercession, of the modes of domination that create and perpetuate this poverty.

The logic of marginalization has an impetus all of its own, particularly as regards the study of modern languages. Here, willy-nilly, the scholar assumes an interdisciplinary stance. While others are confirmed in their specialism, and therefore in their prejudices, by the private castes of the modern academy, the language student finds himself on the margins of a number of disciplines. The disadvantages of such a position are only too obvious, not merely to those more centrally poised – hence the charges of trivialization and methodological naivete – but to the language student himself – hence his touchiness and constitutional insecurity.

And yet and yet . . . By turning the screw of deconstructive analysis, a position of marginality can be transformed into a point of convergence. Such a conviction sustains the present work, which, along with my others, situates itself, suicidally, astride that most controversial and unsurmountable of barriers, between the "arts" and "human sciences." Its very title signals a duality of purpose: an attempt to locate both the work of Jorge Luis Borges and Western ideas on language in their historical context. My aim has been to generate a certain dialectical interplay between what are, in effect, two interlocking plots or narratives, in such a way as to be mutually enlightening and, in combination, disruptive of entrenched, institutionalized preconceptions. It goes without saying that I make no claim to a comprehensive analysis in my treatment either of Borges or of the Western linguistic tradition.

No theoretical work, particularly one which addresses itself directly to the question of the "subject," both transcendental and individual, can avoid confronting the practical problem of how to refer to this category, in simple linguistic terms. By extension, such nouns as "the poet," "the writer," "the reader," "the philosopher," not to mention "man" and "men," raise the same pronominal dilemma. My solution has been to use "it" wherever possible, otherwise "he," to designate any generalized representative, and to use the "he/she" form to refer to actual people. These are, needless to say, ideologically determined conventions, and therefore not entirely satisfactory. However, the alternatives are even less so in the present context, notwithstanding the value of linguistic equalities and even of reversals of binary oppositions for tactical purposes. In particular the generalized use of "he/she" masks not only the institutional situation of inequality but also the formation of the subject, an historical analysis of which is undertaken by the present work. The latter aims not to conjure away the patriarchal basis of Idealism, through the glib manipulation of pronouns, but to understand the actual complexity of its gender base, to expose, in a word, what the idealist *lacks*. Such an understanding is surely the precondition of any genuine transcendence.

I am grateful to Roger Mills for the loan of his type-copied manuscripts of some of Borges' early works, which, as is well known, are extremely difficult to come by in their original printed versions. My thanks also to my colleagues, Laurence Simmons and David Bevan, for their helpful comments; to Daniel Balderston and Gene H. Bell-Villada, readers for UNCSRLL, from whose criticism the final version of this book benefited considerably; and finally to my wife, Sheryl Read, for being so understanding and willing to share the cost of my enthusiasms. Needless to say, I assume full responsibility for the mistakes that remain.

CONTENTS

	Page
ABBREVIATIONS	17
INTRODUCTION	19
I. FROM CLASSICAL SYMBOLS TO MEDIEVAL SIGNS	31
II. PUBLIC USAGE AND PRIVATE ABUSAGE IN THE AGE OF CONFLICT.	54
III. MONSTERS OF ENLIGHTENED REASON	76
IV. THE IDEAL REVOLUTION: ROMANTICISM AND ITS LEGACY	100
V. TO HAVE AND HAVE NOT: MODERNIST LITERATURE AS FETISHISM	122
CONCLUSION	142
BIBLIOGRAPHY	147

ABBREVIATIONS

References in the text to Borges' writings are generally given by an abbreviation of the title, followed by a page reference. Details regarding these writings are to be found in the bibliography.

A	*El Aleph*
CBD	*Crónicas de Busto Domecq* (with Adolfo Bioy Casares)
D	*Discusión*
EC	*Evaristo Carriego*
F	*Ficciones*
H	*El Hacedor*
I	*Inquisiciones*
IA	*El idioma de los argentinos*
IB	*El informe de Brodie*
HE	*Historia de la eternidad*
HI	*Historia universal de la infamia*
LA	*El libro de la arena*
OI	*Otras inquisiciones*
OP	*Obra poética*
P	*Prólogos con un prólogo de prólogos*
SN	*Siete noches*
T	*El tamaño de mi esperanza*

INTRODUCTION

Common sense would suggest that the thicket of critical texts that has grown up around Borges' work since the early '60s must perforce have been flattering and welcome to its author: he doubtless reflected upon the parallel with the Bible and its Cabbalistic commentators – one of his most persistent obsessions. Common sense, however, is well known to set more store by the virtues of social etiquette than by fidelity to fact. It turns its face away from the sordid side of life, from the realities of literary practice, and thereby blinds us to the truth of the relationships not merely between readers, critics and imaginative writers, but also between members within each group respectively. Officially, literary history is a tale of brotherly quest for Truth and of filial homage to writers of genius. Unofficially, it tells of fratricide and patricide. In the case of Borges, this doctrine of double-truth is particularly poignant, since what is denied, namely the internecine strife, is thematically and otherwise so fundamental to his work.

Each author writes with an ideal reader in mind, in which regard Borges has been a good deal more specific than most: "The ideal reader of my works would be a person who greatly resembles me, one who would not look for too many intentions in what I have written but would abandon himself to reading" (Barrenechea, 150). The author's anxieties are palpable, and with good reason: the reader, after all, has subversive potential. To look for too many intentions is to privilege the text, which thereby threatens to eclipse the sovereign presence of the author-itarian subject. The latter, ever ready to assert his own desires, consumes the outside, as other, by constructing a work so perfect and complete as to render the reader entirely otiose. The result is a neo-Kantian monism, which can only conceive of dialogue as a form of monologue. For with whom other than with himself can the idealist talk? There is just no exit from his solipsistic revery to the *Ding an sich.*

The mirror relationship between author and reader, it is apparent, involves not merely elements of fullness and union, but also of antagonism and conflict. For his part, the author seeks both to impress, to seduce, and at the same time to dominate the reader. Beneath the benign facade, we discern in Borges a patriarch intent upon intimidating his passive, feminine partner in a copulatory act. Predictably, Borges, *qua* reader, is an ideal role model: "El hecho estético es algo tan evidente, tan inmediato, tan indefinible como el amor, el sabor de la fruta, el agua. Sentimos la poesía como sentimos una montaña o una bahía. Si la sentimos inmediatamente, ¿a qué diluirla en otras palabras, que sin duda serán más débiles que nuestros sentimientos?" (SN, 107-8). It is the reader who is on trial, whose adequacy is in question. Is he able to measure up to the work, to accommodate its phallic fullness? Obviously not, if this reader is also a critic, insofar as critical discourse, by definition, is bound to fall short of its object. Just as the Godhead cannot be touched by human language, so the poem is invulnerable to commentary. To read adequately is to surrender the critical will-to-power in exchange for an absolute openness to the other.

Appropriately, since all fraternities are secretly homosexual by nature, literature becomes in idealist terms a gentleman's club, with a strictly limited membership. The vast majority of people are excluded. We should not ask why this is so, or how it came about: there are just some questions a gentleman does not ask. "Creo que la poesía es algo que se siente, y si ustedes no sienten la poesía, si no tienen sentimiento de belleza, [. . .] el autor no ha escrito para ustedes" (SN, 107). Conditions of membership include the suspension of all personal beliefs. One's principal duty in polite society is to *feel,* not to *think:* "Soy casi incapaz de pensamiento abstracto [. . .]. [H]ablar abstractamente de poesía [. . .] es una forma del tedio o de la haraganería" (SN, 108). Far from hiding his anti-speculative bias, the idealist positively flaunts it. He moves instinctively to inhibit any attempt to expose literature to the real world. His own critical discourse lays claim to being the ultimate in immanent analysis, resisting any temptation to "go outside the text." The reader is encouraged to recreate or re-experience the work strictly "in its own terms."

As bourgeois liberalism enters into crisis, so too does the "free," autonomous subject by which it is sustained. Borges is the first to register its insecurity, to concede that a work exceeds by far the author's intentions, conscious or otherwise, and that its interpretation lies "entirely in the hands of the reader" (Barrenechea, 152). The problematics of authorship will figure increasingly in his work, along with the disengagement of literature from reality. It is a concession of which the New Critic is quick to take advantage, given his overwhelming need to depoliticize the ideologically highly charged atmosphere of North American academies in the 1960s.[1]

In any agonic conflict, in literature as in life, the roles are infinitely permutable. Accordingly, whereas the neo-idealist moves from the text to something anterior to it, namely what the author meant, the New Critic discovers in the text a means of privileging his own role at the expense of the author. He boasts his fidelity to an immanent form, in the Platonic or Aristotelian sense of an Idea or Form to which the work aspires teleologically. Reassembled and reconstructed in critical commentary, the work exhibits an unsuspected unity and harmony. Given the imperfections of the material, corruptible world, a degree of failure on the artist's part may seem inevitable. However, the critic, in his own newly discovered authoritative capacity, is a perfectionist, and, like all perfectionists, unforgiving. Pontification comes easily to him: clearly, he lectures, the author could have done better. It is now the critic's turn to intimidate the writer.

But the game of interchanging images is endless. The body of the text, stripped of its flesh by the critic, is itself a spectre. "Interpretation is repetition, but a strange repetition that *says more by saying less*" (Machery, 76). And that, turning the screw of paradox, in saying less, actually says more: commentaries on Borges outgrow the original narratives, which, shrewdly, are themselves models of economy. Economy should here be understood in the Neoplatonic sense of the term. In other words, simplicity and brevity are the hallmark of the Platonic archetype and signal an increasing spirituality on a vertical axis. While the writer ascends to celestial heights, the critic succumbs to the drag of material verbiage; it is *he* who spills his words immoderately, and, in the process, accedes to the status of mere reflection.

---

[1] See Bell-Villada, 273.

Without the controlling presence of the author, words tend to run riot, arousing all kinds of hidden fears in orthodox Academia. Anarchy, linguistic and otherwise, can be averted only through recourse to an implicit intentionalism, "a quest for what it *appeared* the author had had in mind" (Belsey, 16). After all, the prime consideration is not the excision of the author but of the social and historical outside: "The stories of *El Aleph* in no way reflect the changed political circumstances in which they were written" (Cohen, 66). Thus, studies of Borges continue to foster attention to textual detail, and to slide incessantly from the text to its source in the mind of the writer, at the expense of those broader considerations that unavoidably raise the uncomfortable issue of praxis. Borges' work "is concerned not with advocating changes in social conditions, but with investigating the human condition. It is in the best sense exploratory. It stimulates the reader not to act or react, but to think" (Shaw [1976], 76). Conservative Academia gives the nod of approval. Borges becomes the darling of university campuses.

Needless to say, the New Critic is unable to theorize his own strategical moves: the very loss of nerve that decides them also dissuades him from scrutinizing his own methodology, for which reason he remains blind not only to his own ideological circumstances but to those of the text. Like the idealist, the New Critic assumes that the text determines its context of interpretation. Other critical voices are disparaged as incorrigibly biased and reductive, the exponents of so much dull "jargon." The ideological implications of Borges' stories and of their reception are never allowed to cloud their "intrinsic worth." Thus, for example, while (to his credit) untypically sensitive to Borges' prejudices and disparaging of his illiberal comments – such as his support for the Bay of Pigs invaders and demand for the execution of Régis Debray – Bell-Villada yet maintains that "None of this diminishes Borges's stature as a literary artist" (Bell-Villada, 275). Amongst New Critics, canon construction never figures as a subject of serious debate.

New Criticism survives, and continues to flourish as the underpinning of much Borgesian scholarship, but was superceded in the 1950s, at least among the initiated, by a more business-like, scientistic kind of myth criticism, associated with the name of Northrop Frye. While continuing to resist commodification – hence his withdrawal from social, historical existence into the realm of art – the myth critic surrenders his negative impulse to become a servant of a bureaucratized society.[2] He theorizes the displacement of the autonomous individual in favour of a communal subject. The abandonment of history is clearly apparent in Frye's cyclic model of evolving *mythoi*, which is reminiscent of Borges' fictionalized "history of eternity." Both critic and author envisage the writer as the function of a tradition which transcends him and, as it were, speaks through him.

The conception of individuation as occurring within the system, not as prior to it, undeniably represents a serious challenge to liberal humanism. At the same time, myth criticism is less innovative than it would appear to be at first sight. Indeed, Frye (like Borges) consistently betrays his allegiance to the tradition of German idealism. Rather than avoiding solipsism, he merely transfers it from the writer to the system. Discussion about the autotelic status of the individual work is thereby extended to Literature itself. As Frances Wyers Weber illustrates, the consequences for "practical criticism" are slight: "the work of art gives meaning to experience only if it first functions aesthetically, that is, in the case of literature, as an autonomous verbal structure in which all meaning is inward and reflexive. The poet is not concerned with referential meaning" (Wyers Weber, 125n7).[3]

Not everyone, however, can share the equanimity with which mythic criticism views the radical dissociation of literary discourse from a contingent reality. The task of reconciling literature's mimetic responsibilities with its transcendental pretensions was raised with particular urgency by Murray Krieger (Krieger, 199 and passim). The Hispanist certainly has good reason to respond to Krieger's concern. What, after all, can mythic criticism make of a writer such as Borges, whose fictions "persistently undermine their own independence and organic wholeness" (Wyers Weber, 126n7). It is not merely Borges that is at issue: "Fiction in the Cervantine tradition, which takes as its central theme the problem of illusion and reality, purposefully destroys itself as an inviolate hermetic orb. One might ask how such a work can be considered centripetal and self-contained."

Krieger was influential in channelling American criticism from the idealist celebration of an organically functioning discourse, ca-

---

[2] See Fekete, 127-9.
[3] For further discussion, see Hart, 501-2.

pable of authentic access to the real, towards a conservative fictionalism the ultimate feat of which is to validate a "fiction" in which, from the very beginning, we do not believe. Krieger found in Wallace Stevens the perfect exponent of this ironic brand of existentialism.[4] He might well have looked towards Borges, both as a kindred spirit, whose development corresponds closely with his own, and as a perfect example of the ironist. In his mature fiction, Borges foregrounds an imaginative world whose order is our only reality, from which he steps into a real world which is profoundly irrational, chaotic and, the demands of logic notwithstanding, unknowable.

Frye's structuralism is contemporary with classical French structuralism, which itself has been determine by American New Criticism.[5] However, the distinguishing feature of classical structuralism, namely the notion of identities differentially defined as opposed to conferred through individual substance, is lacking in the Anglo-Saxon tradition. Significantly, Hispanic thematic structuralism is at pains to distinguish itself from its continental counterpart.[6] Clearly, concessions had to be made to a firmly entrenched, native empiricism. No "practical critic" could rest easy with a French structuralism which, in its extremity, brackets both the objective world and the author. Hence the sense of outrage occasioned by the structuralist John Sturrock, who "ignores remarks by Borges which run counter to the thrust of his own argument" (Shaw [1978], 347). This comment indicates the extent to which Sturrock offers a *strong* interpretation of the text. The structuralist's main allegiance is to his master code, language, in terms of which Borges is rewritten. The traditional critic, blissfully unaware of his own master code, is shocked by what he discerns as a blatant Nietzschean will-to-power and a clear case of reductionism.

The major challenge to Borges and his art, however, was to come not from structuralism, with which, as a writer obsessed with language, Borges has some affinity, but from two modes of thought deeply antagonistic to his own ideology, that is to say, psychoanalysis and Marxism. Borges rejects the former as a discipline obsessed with "a few rather unpleasant facts," whose founder was a "charlatan" or "madman" (Burgin, 109). Similarly, the structuralist critic

---

[4] See Lentricchia, 240-2.
[5] See Fekete, 129; Williams (1979), 337-8.
[6] See Pring-Mill, 370n4.

swerves at the crucial moment when psychology and psychoanalysis rear their ugly heads: "The pattern, as always, is suspiciously neat" (Sturrock, 75). Such opposition, it needs to be said, is not entirely unjustified. Matamoro's debunking of Borges' Oedipal fixation remains finally hamstrung by the whole problematic of psychologizing authors, not to mention the critic's curiously oppressive brand of ego psychology that serves the established bourgeois order as effectively as does structuralism itself (Matamoro, 52-53 and passim). Moreover, although in a sense all abstraction necessarily belies a complex reality (such as that of the individual life), psychoanalysis lays itself open to the more radical charge of reductionism. Even a life as apparently mundane as Borges' threatens constantly to overflow the boundaries imposed by the castration seme, and the repetitive recasting of his stories in terms of a simplified model of the Oedipal myth, while initially revealing, proves finally numbing and constrictive. With reason, Freud himself warned of the danger of "wild" analyses.

At the same time, however, psychoanalysis attacks structuralism at its most vulnerable point, namely its assumption of the notion of a unified and consistent subject. This transcendental subject, by definition, would escape scientific analysis, functioning as the repository of the structure. It is the virtue of psychoanalysis that it opens up this hidden human mind to scrutiny, maps its terrain, and charts its development. It provides, in short, a theory of the subject-in-process, without which the critic is unable to account for the "primal loss" that is fundamental to Borges' fiction. The radical limitations of structuralism are, in contrast, only too apparent: paired characters hate each other for "apparently frivolous" reasons, psychologically frivolous that is (Sturrock, 170, 171). They hate each other because they are rivals; their rivalry gives rise to fictions. Beyond this simple postulation of binary oppositions the structuralist is unable to progress. His limitations derive directly from his methodology. Structuralism's tendency to operate in terms of fully finished subjects and objects is confirmed by Sturrock's attempts to resolve internal contradictions. Borges is "absolutely a Classicist," the "complete Realist." But the truth is that a strong element of Romanticism (as opposed to Classicism) remained intact in Borges throughout his career, and that a writer who so consistently occupies the margins between fiction and reality must be allowed more than a passing fascination with Nominalism (notwithstanding his Realism). It is not the business of the critic to repress psychic conflict but to elucidate its complex etiology.

In a sense, of course, such elucidation is what Borges' own fiction is about, as is confirmed by his relationship to post-structuralism. When the transcendental subject begins to fragment, under the pressure of monopoly capitalism, it was to Borges that scholars looked to illustrate their concerns: "[Borges] simply dispenses with the least obvious, but most compelling, of necessities; he does away with the *site,* the mute ground upon which it is possible for entities to be juxtaposed" (Foucault [1970], xvii). Foucault is here referring to Borges' Chinese encyclopedia, which, with its disordered orderliness, effectively demolishes the whole rationalist *episteme* of the classical age. Significantly, much post-structuralist thought involves a re-reading of the seminal texts of idealism, to which Borges is himself so indebted. Even Julia Kristeva's materialism proceeds by reading such texts against the grain, and finds in Borges' "infamy" one of the few concepts that can plumb that *abjection* through which the subject establishes a boundary between itself and matter and upon which its identity correspondingly depends. For infamy hints darkly of the "rampancy, boundlessness, the unthinkable, the untenable, the unsymbolizable [. . .], the untiring repetition of a drive, which, propelled by an initial loss, does not cease wandering, unsated, deceived, warped, until it finds its only stable object – death" (Kristeva [1982], 23).

One last agon remains to be acted out, specifically that between Borges and the Marxist critic, who ambitiously claims to provide the ultimate conceptual horizon of literature. The battle lines are drawn. Borges insists provocatively: "I am an antagonist of littérature engagée" (Giovanni *et al.,* 59). Matamoro responds by dismissing Borges as the spokesman for a bourgeois ahistoricism imbibed from the British imperial circles to which, by birth, he belonged (Matamoro, 19, 147-50). We need not linger, by way of assessing Borges' contribution to the debate, on his own embarrassingly ill-informed, reactionary pronouncements on political and economic matters.[7] Suffice it to say that they reveal an Idealism far transcending the ludic dimensions to which he otherwise pretends. More deserving of attention are the major theoretical problems raised by the Lukacsian brand of Marxist aesthetics deployed by Matamoro. The

---

[7] Cf. Bell-Villada, 23, 267; Franco, 57-58.

most notorious concerns the suitability of the norms of nineteenth-century realism as the touchstone for literary evaluation. While they enable Matamoro to expose the ideological sources of Borges' sceptical ennui, these norms are themselves a product of the same bourgeois culture that the critic would otherwise denounce. As such, they preclude a sympathetic understanding of the mind-boggling radicalism of Borges' modernist texts, whose technically subversive practices are reminiscent of the "estrangement effect" seen by other Marxist critics as indispensable to a genuinely revolutionary art.[8] To these shortcoming we must add Matamoro's failure to reflect critically upon the troubled relationship between Marxism and psychoanalysis, upon the combined contributions of which he bases his assault upon Borges. How (we wonder) does he reconcile his Marxism with a movement whose "reduction to the body" masks the political ambitions of the bourgeoisie?

The present work seeks to distance itself theoretically from the text under analysis, so as more effectively to articulate its ideology. Accordingly, we argue the need to press beyond Marxist versions of Borges' artistic development which contrast an early radical, creole with a later imperialist phase.[9] Such narratives are only superficially different – for "imperialist" read "universalist" – from their bourgeois counterparts, and, through their very proximity to Borges' texts, are as misleading as they are enlightening. What we demand is a more mediated explanation which accounts for the conservative elements of Borges' early dominant Romanticism, and the Romantic elements in his subsequent conservative classicism.

One of the few writers to have risen seriously to the challenge posed by the geniune complexity of Borges' work is Jean Franco. Franco justifiably reproaches a left-wing criticism which has largely confined itself to *ad hominem* debate when it has not simply attempted to reduce Borges' work to its social determinants. As she rightly argues: "The disadvantage of this [approach] is that it denies the very capability – the abstraction from concrete situations – which give the fictions their power. Yet it is precisely mastery, and the abstraction mastery is based on, that demand analysis" (Franco, 53). This emphasis on abstraction, however, if pursued undialectically, poses its own dangers. Symptomatically, it is to Foucault, not

---

[8] See Fredric Jameson, "Reflections in Conclusion," in Bloch *et al.*, 202 ff.
[9] See, for example, Fernández Retamar, 44.

to Marx, that Franco looks to reconnect Borges with the real world of class struggle, power and the reproduction of material life (75). But Foucault has already confessed his admiration for Borges, a fact which should alert us, if nothing else does, to the rampantly idealist basis of his own genealogy.[10] It is to neutralize the possibility of such idealist contamination that the present work attempts to *historicize* Borges' capacity for abstraction.

In this more mediated explanation polemic can, and should, continue to play a key role. For example, a Marxist should not flinch from exposing the transitive nature of any concept of "value."[11] Tactically, he must invalidate the bourgeois manoeuvre which enables the critic to esteem a particular author independently of the latter's ideological situation. Once the partisan nature of bourgeois literary history is established, and the traditional canon recast, it becomes possible to present Borges as the author of "slightly immortal books," which are in themselves "the painful testimony of a class with no way out" (Fernández Retamar, 48). Moreover, he is bound to insist, however outrageously (from the standpoint of bourgeois criticism), that Borges' portrayal of cosmic alienation of essential man simply rationalizes the degraded nature of social existence under capitalism, and that his "fictions" are symptomatic – hence their appeal – of the individual's absolute solitude within a consumer society.

The opportunity for a Marxist intervention in Borgesian criticism is, it seems to me, particularly favourable in view of recent moves within liberal criticism against some of its own most cherished traditional shibboleths. Undertakings have been made to be "attentive to historical and political context," even to the extent of "transgressing what formalist critics of whatever variety would consider the limits of the text" (Balderston, 332-3). It is no longer deemed sufficient to *thrill* to Borges' work, to respond to it as if it were "una mera actividad lúdica" (Molloy, 13). We are called to a more serious critical enterprise, which refuses to domesticate rogue elements in the text.

Undoubtedly, these developments connect, in their ultimate determinations, with the direct intrusion of socio-economic and political forces into the Academy. The challenge of a cultural Thatch-

---

[10] Cf. Dews, 171 ff.
[11] See Bennett, 172-3.

erism-Reaganism unsympathetic to the humanities has aroused not merely a pervasive sense of anger but also of guilt on the part of more liberal academics. Before their very eyes, the programme of universal education has been first compromised and finally abandoned, along with all but the pretence of a genuinely democratic society.

It is precisely at this point, at which the pressing need is felt to reconsider Borges' much vaunted *irrealidad* and ludic pretensions, that Marxism must spell out what it is to link artistic specificity to the real, complex relations of actual societies. For it is at this point that doubts easily beset the liberal, when he fears accusations from his more conservative colleagues. In a sudden loss of nerve, the traditional tone of complacency, characteristic of much academic criticism, threatens to return and channel transgressive readings not into demands for social liberation but into the simple recharging of a bankrupt Institution and the preservation of its classics. In a regressive call for oral satisfaction as opposed to the sadistic pleasures of anal aggressivity ("una lectura eliminativa"), the critical experience of irritation is surrendered for the savouring of finely textured morsels, seasoned with a touch of subversiveness ("Detenerse en lo que se incorpora: en el puro placer físico" [Molloy, 9]). For discerning palates such textual jouissance is a "necessary" indulgence.

It is important to recall the capacity of Academia, however moribund, particularly in its most intellectually inert quarters, to absorb radical discourse. In the snakes and ladders of academic life, there is more than one set of serpentine jaws waiting to swallow unwary travellers – feminist, deconstructionist, psychoanalytic baggage and all – and to deposit them in a square embarrassingly proximate to their beginnings in orthodoxy. It behoves the Marxist to recall if not the hunger of the Third World then at least the unpalatable stodge of those whose lot it is to labour; to ensure moreover that his own critical discourse properly analyzes the specific relationships through which texts are produced and move, and thereby to set the terms of reference for all future discussion. This means in the case of Borges addressing himself to the precarious situation of an Argentinian bourgeoisie threatened by a growing mass of proletarian immigrants and the dissolution of individual structures in the critical belated transition in a dependent colony from industrial to monopoly capitalism.

The dangers of such an approach, including in particular a crude economism, are only too obvious. While seeking therefore to preserve something of the "shock" value that characterized Marxist criticism in its vulgar forms, I will aim in the present work to respect the complex correspondence between the art work and the sociological and historical circumstances of its composition; in the interests of which I will assume a less domineering and, in the end, less imperialistic perspective on art, seeking to disrupt, not simply to reverse, that master-slave relationship which, formerly, has cast the critic as a subject who exerts authority over a literary object.

Within these parameters, we will argue that, while it contained elements of Romantic progressivism, the idealist criticism that Borges recommends, as distinct from positivist criticism, was part of a more general Romantic reaction to the dehumanization of late capitalism. In the twentieth century, when it was opposed by structuralism, neo-idealism was expounded by a middle-class intelligentsia nostalgic for the organicism of an earlier period. Accordingly, it flourished as a pre-urban movement in less industrialized countries, such as Germany, Italy, Spain and thence to the South American republics. From this tradition emerged some of the most effective critiques of modern civilization. Its exponents spoke eloquently of the need to withdraw from the capitalist market, in order to preserve those emotional qualities banished by consumerism. Resisting the bureaucratization of society, they managed to preserve, although in an attenuated form, the negative, critical force of early Romanticism. Finally, however, neo-idealism shows itself to be an irrational conservatism that deals only in *ideas* of social process. Lacking any political strategy, it gradually loses its cutting edge, and is transformed into a positive movement supportive of the very technologism against which it was originally a reaction. Its categories – in particular, those of the "individual" and "society" – are themselves the product of capitalist thought.

CHAPTER I

FROM CLASSICAL SYMBOLS TO MEDIEVAL SIGNS

I

"[L]os nombres no son símbolos arbitrarios sino parte vital de lo que definen" (OI, 223). Borges is here summarizing a magical, primitivist view of language. We are not, of course, overtly invited to embrace it, or to assume that Borges embraces it. Such anti-conventionalist sentiments are clearly entertained, at least in part, in a spirit of play, an instance of that gleefully outrageous attitudinizing so typical of the writer's work. After all, as we shall see, one would not be hard pressed to find statements by him elsewhere that contradict the "naturalist" standpoint. At the same time, however, its obsessive recurrence betrays a basic seriousness of intent, suggestive of a profound attachment to the pre-Socratic unity of *logos,* in which language was seen as at one with the order of the natural world and with social institutions and practice.

Subsequently shattered by the development of "civilization," this unity perdures (as Borges learned from such anthropologists as J. G. Fraser) in the belief in taboo and secret names, phenomena characteristic of primitive cultures, such as those of Ancient Egyptians and of the Australian Aborigines. The adult, civilized being – here Fritz Mauthner was Borges' source – never escapes their reach: in the twilight zones of our thoughts, where megalomania and paranoia are rampant, words continue to kill and enslave, through the power of calumny, perjury, and insult (OI, 223-4). This is the world of magic, in which thoughts are omnipotent and words possess a thaumaturgic force, and in which the individual is caught within a web of hidden correspondences or lines of energy that bind his body to the universe at large: "[. . .] la magia es la coronación o pesadilla de lo causal, no su contradicción. El milagro no es menos forastero en ese universo que en el de los astrónomos. Todas las leyes naturales lo rigen, y otras imaginarias. Para el supersticioso, hay una necesaria conexión no sólo entre un balazo y un muerto, sino entre un muerto y una maltratada efigie de cera" (D, 89). We enter upon it through an act of truancy from the reality-principle, for example, in the cult of astrology, or, as Borges insists, in fiction.

Thus, paradoxically, the passage to civilization corresponds with a break, preserved ontogenetically in the Fall from the primeval world of infantile bliss:

> [. . .] Ya es impreciso
> En la memoria el claro Paraíso,
> Pero yo sé que existe y que perdura,
> Aunque no para mí. La terca tierra
> Es mi castigo y la incestuosa guerra
> De Caínes y Abeles y su cría.
> Y, sin embargo, es mucho haber amado,
> Haber sido feliz, haber tocado
> El viviente Jardín, siquiera un día.   (OP, 253)

The frustration of the writer is that finally his fictional tigers lack the reality of the real thing, or of those that linger from childhood in his dreams (H, 17-18).

Such nostalgia for a pre-lapsarian unity has its materialist possibilities. Walter Benjamin notoriously found in the Edenic word a language incarnate that "sank its roots into sensuous practice" (Eagleton [1981], 151). Here the Marxist critic gives a dialectical twist to the opposition between word and body that pits Scriptural exegesis against Saussure's bourgeois notion of the arbitrary signed. Significantly, however, Benjamin looks to Baroque art to reinstate the matter of which post-lapsarian idioms have been cleansed. In contrast Borges sees in Góngora the antagonist *par excellence* of the classic purity which he himself prefers and practises.

Even in Benjamin, Biblical hermeneutics leads, as far as a genuine Marxism is concerned, to a "grisly caricature" of Edenic materiality and to a flight from history which gives evidence of the inescapably idealist basis of his thinking (19). In Borges the communion with the concrete – symbolized by those fat cats that smilingly preside over his fictions –[1] will remain confessedly outside not

---

[1] See, for example, "El Sur" and "Deutsches Requiem."

merely history but also time itself, leaving the Argentinian writer hopelessly compromised in terms of the arbitrary sign and the bourgeois ideology with which, in the modern period, this sign has been inextricably entwined.

All gardens have a wall. So do cities and empires, as a means of defence against the anal drives that constantly threaten to decompose the symbolic. Enigmatic, feminine, anterior to judgement, these drives constitute what Kristeva has called the *semiotic,* which subverts the rational order of syntax.[2] They introduce the elements of contingency and chance of which, in its magical forms, language is cleansed: the really demonic is the fallen world of disorder and chaos. This explains why the mark of civilized man is his obsession with anality. In his desperation, he would purify language ("quisiéramos volverlo tan límpido" [IA, 182]). Life becomes one long evacuation. The excrement drops away from us, in a constant postponement of the day when we, as bodies, drop away also: ashes to ashes, dust to dust.

After all, the stakes are high: our very identities are threatened by the return of the repressed. The Great Wall of China and the burning of books by the Emperor Shin Huang Ti are, as Borges explains, instances of "barreras mágicas" against death (OI, 10). But, in the irony that overtakes all flight from death, immortal form is deathly form. The sublimations of civilized man drain the magic out of the body, in accordance with the dialectic of life against death. They betray "man's incapacity to live in the body, which is also his incapacity to die" (Brown [1968], 265). Civilization thereby reproduces in its exalted forms the very image of that primal inertia to which all life strives to return. Without the abjection of the body, we cannot be; yet by a perverse paradox, this break involves the death of the soma, which burdens man with a sense of non-being.

The thetic break that divides the symbolic from the semiotic assumes many guises according to circumstance. For the Argentinian it marks the division between civilization and barbarity, a singularly clear-cut polarization, that separates Buenos Aires from the interior. This is why, for Borges, Evaristo Carriego epitomizes man's contradictory nature. He sits astride the divide: "La irrealidad de las orillas es más sutil: deriva de su provisorio carácter, de la doble gravitación de la llanura chacarera o ecuestre y de la calle de altos, de la

---

[2] See Kristeva [1984], 49-50; Stallybrass and White, 167-8.

propensión de sus hombres a considerarse del campo o de la ciudad, jamás orilleros" (EC, 94-95).[3] In the suburbs, a site of transition, all contradictions are neutralized, in such a way that the encroachment of the country upon the city is blocked.

The same divide also splits the inner psyche into two, opposing conscious to unconscious, signifier to signified, ego to id. Into the domain of the barbarous other, European man ejects all his own private fears and fantasies, that he would disown but which return to plague him again, only to be re-ejected into that outside which is also an inside. The archetypal Faustian figure, he is perforce a homeless denizen of the margins: "La orilla es imprecisa, sometida sin descanso a las fluctuaciones de la marea y de la tierra que cede o avanza" (Tamayo and Ruiz-Díaz, 51).

Rather than the shore-line, however, the city wall best symbolizes the primary bar. To found a city, as the *Conquistadores* often demonstrated, is to demarcate its body by tracing its boundaries in the sand. Thereafter the city is always a body politic. Borges' family belonged to the head, namely the oligarchy, sons and grand-sons of landowning gentlemen who masterminded the War of Independence, *ex-terminated* the Indians, and opposed the barbarian *caudillos* who sought in turn to *liquidate* them. This old-fashioned liberalism tolerates experimental subjectivism, such as Borges' *ultraísta* poetry of the 1920s, but understandably grows fearful in the face of a burgeoning proletariat.

History proved its fears justified. For it was on the backs of the newly urbanized masses that Perón swept to power, bringing ruin to the traditional bourgeoisie.[4] The latter felt more affinity with

---

[3] See also Tamayo and Ruiz-Díaz, 50-51.

[4] The inability of the Argentinian and Socialist Parties to capitalize on the massive reservoir of proletarian labour – Argentina was the only South American country to show conditions potentially favourable for a class struggle along European lines – has often been noted by historians. For example, James Petras writes: "A major factor conditioning attitudes towards Peronism in Argentina was a double failure of the traditional Left. First, it failed to organize the majority of unskilled industrial workers and therefore was unable to provide tangible benefits to the great mass of the working class. The Communist and Socialist parties were based in craft unions and isolated plant unions, highly fragmented and generally ineffective, leaving the mass of workers out of the range of their organizations. This undercut any ideological appeal based on class analysis. Second, the traditional Left could not relate to the basic social conflicts within the country since it sought alliances with traditional parliamentary groups and tied itself to the foreign policy needs of other countries – the Socialist Party to those of the United States, the Communist Party

Parisians than with the migrant peons and immigrant labour, whom it envisaged as so much contemptible matter, to be flushed away in the appropriate manner "a través de la iluminación que desciende desde el empíreo europeo" (Viñas [1964], 47). Borges was one of the victims of popularism, finding himself no longer cushioned by a private income and a sinecure.[5]

But if reality saw the barbarians enjoying political power, in literature the sacred space of the city is re-affirmed: both cities and fictions "[are] the extension of culture into the territory of nature" (Sturrock, 100n5). Classicism re-draws the boundaries; art marks off a private space, uncontaminated by dirt. Within literature, the bourgeoisie could feel safe. Safe, but not immune to the attractions of the outside. Civilization, after all, is spun out of man's backside, through sublimation, and the dirt that is continually pressed beyond the city limits returns to infect the suburban precincts. Enclosed within the city, within a library, Borges is fascinated by the very image that he abhors, that of the rural bosses and the strong-arm men of Palermo. In particular the *compadre* figures as the archetypal plebeian, who will antagonistically confront Borges in his fictions and – this was after all the heyday of Perón – annihilate him. A timid literator, Borges has the feeling of never having lived, save vicariously through his violent protagonists.[6]

II

The primitive artist aspires not to imitate but to make. He assumes a capacity to exert a magical influence upon the world, on the basis of a hidden identity between the artefact and the object which serves as a model. Greek art, in its revolutionary insistence upon the need to portray reality exactly, presupposes a loss of this causal link, as a result of which the art object is reduced to the status of a pale reflection of the real.[7] Primitivism survives in the myth of Pygmalion, in the light of which we are able to understand the

---

to those of Russia" (Petras, 83). See Caballero (44-45) for the Stalinization imposed by the Comintern, involving of course a compromise with Western capitalist powers.
  [5] See Rodríguez Monegal (1978), 394 ff.
  [6] See Rodríguez Monegal (1971), 21.
  [7] See Gombrich, 80 ff.

sorrow (to the point of manic depression) that all artists feel after the exhilaration of actually completing their work. Who has not known that grey feeling of the "morning after," when we face the product of our previous day's labour? "Suddenly the ignored gaps and fragmentation and the apparent chaos of undifferentiation push into consciousness" (Ehrenzweig, 118). We are overwhelmed by a sense of anal disgust, caused by the residue of matter that escapes formal transubstantiation.

Borges explores the pygmalion myth in "Parábola del palacio," in which artefact and original object, as antagonistic mirror images, engage in a battle over Being. This Being is conditional upon the possession of the original maternal object, symbolized by the palace. At the foot of the penultimate (phallic) tower, the poet recites a poem which eclipses the emperor's palace. The castration seme (*"¡Me has arrebatado el palacio!"* [H, 57]) generates conflicting conclusions to the narrative. According to one, the rebellious son-poet is eliminated by the father-emperor, his poem thereby accorded a purely nominal status; whereas in the second version, the poem replaces the palace, which now becomes a mere reflexion of the verbal artefact.

In a sense, the outcome is – note the term – immaterial. Of fundamental importance is what both narrative versions presuppose, namely the decisive loss of the pre-Socratic unity of the logos. From a primary social division between master and slave, between those that *think* and those that *labour*, other distinctions follow. The conscious mind stands over against material reality, just as in the *Cratylus* the "word" is opposed to the "thing." Debate no longer questions the fact of such dichotomies but focuses upon their ramifications.[8] By positing as given a reality of pure Forms, it burdens all subsequent investigators with a metaphysical bias that they automatically assume, along with all the rest of the idealist baggage so much in evidence in, amongst others, Borges:

> Si (como el griego afirma en el Cratilo)
> El nombre es arquetipo de la cosa,
> En las letras de *rosa* está la rosa
> Y todo el Nilo en la palabra *Nilo*.   (OP, 147)

---

[8] See Williams (1977), 22.

Needless to say, this naturalist thesis was opposed by a conventionalist thesis, the latter reflecting the loss of the primitive commune and the corresponding fragmentation of society. That language plays a vital role in the process of production in any society is a truism whose consequences are commonly forgotten or ignored. The naturalist thesis preserves, albeit in abstract form, the knowledge of a stage in which all men were actively engaged in labour on the rest of nature, and therefore participated in the wholeness of man engaged in his own becoming. The transformation of the economic base of society which allows the privileged withdrawal of certain groups deprives these same groups of the knowledge of language as it functions within lived and living relationships, relationships which "*make all formal meanings significant and substantial, in a world of reciprocal reference which moves, as it must, beyond the signs*" (Williams [1977], 168). To the contemplative, passive philosopher-scientist, living off the social surplus, the sign necessarily appears to be arbitrary. He projects onto language his own experience of dehumanization.

Given his own comparable status, the bourgeois idealist of the twentieth century enjoys that social distance which inevitably inclines him also to the concept of arbitrariness. As Borges, who was such an idealist, argues: "Aunque Platón sabía que había otros idiomas, los otros eran bárbaros. Para él sólo existía el idioma griego. Entonces no le parecía tan absurdo como a nosotros que hubiera una relación entre las palabras y sus sentidos [. . .]. En cambio ahora sabemos demasiada filosofía para creer eso y podemos pensar que las palabras son símbolos arbitrarios" (Sosnowski, 74-75n101). For the bourgeoisie, freedom, at root commercial, lies within convention, within a city clearly demarcated from nature. At the same time, however, idealism marks a point of resistance against the dehumanizing effects of advanced capitalism, as epitomized by the structuralist's view of the arbitrary sign. This explains Borges' reluctance to relinquish the naturalist thesis: "no deja de ser significativo que hablemos de contar un cuento y de contar hasta mil" (P, 167). Of course, idealism can only ever institute an *idea* of nature, insofar as it represses the body, along with the material conditions of language.

The above qualification is of fundamental importance. It explains why in "Las ruinas circulares," Borges' most extensive treatment of the Pygmalion theme, the "powerful names" uttered by the magician instate only an ideal body. The ghosts that he constructs required only "un mínimo de mundo visible" (F, 62). The labour of construction is banished from the realm of thought: "le infundió el olvido total de sus años de aprendizaje" (67). Necessarily, this inflicts upon the idealist subject a problem of being. The paling, taciturn magician possesses a spectral body "consagrado a la única tarea de dormir y soñar" (63). Gradually, all libidinous contact with reality is severed: "Percibía con cierta palidez los sonidos y formas del universo" (67).

Of course, this retreat is, paradoxically, conducted in the interests of a more authentic existence. Capitalism despises art; it condemns the craftsman to oblivion, replacing him eventually with automata that will more effectively "mind" his machines. Literature remains the last major point of resistance to consumerism. The creative writer dreams of stealing the secret of fire from the gods, like Prometheus. But Prometheus, he should have remembered, was punished for his daring by symbolic castration. The magician also is castrated, though he does not realize it at first. He is not a body but a thought, in the mind of another, caught up in a process of infinite regress which reproduces in miniature the very structure of the nightmarish society from which the writer flees.

Necessarily, the binary oppositions, primarily that between nature and convention, remain unresolved and unresolvable, at least within the parameters of idealism. In an Aristotelian mode Borges condemns "el inmóvil y terrible museo de los arquetipos platónicos," and rejects a world which is "quieto, monstruoso y clasificado" (HE, 16). For the Platonists, and for those capable of Platonizing, he continues, the form is the ultimate reality, but for us mortals, who cannot forget our bodies, "la última y firme realidad de las cosas es la materia" (17). From the standpoint of an Aristotelianism traditionally interpreted as heralding a return to material reality, Borges categorically dismisses the Platonic realm of the Ideal: "Hemos examinado una eternidad que es más pobre que el mundo" (23).

But the reality to which Borges would return is a capitalist society based on estranged labour and an exchange value, money, from which all individuality has been extinguished, and which, in turn, provokes a reaction. Needless to say, in the absence of a viable alternative, involving the revolutionary transformation of society, such a reaction can only take one form, namely the reinstatement of that macabre realm of Platonic forms. This realm, itself a symptom of social alienation, promotes a generic experience which is more intense that the concrete: "De chico, veraneando en el norte de la provincia, la llanura redonda y los hombres que mateaban en la cocina me interesaron, pero mi felicidad fue terrible cuando supe que ese redondel era 'pampa,' y esos varones, 'gauchos'" (HE, 21n1).

Interestingly, Borges records his pseudo-mystical insight in a footnote. As deconstructionists have taught us, footnotes often contain the unwanted matter that is ripe for reinstatement into the textual superstructure. This particular aside demonstrates just how easy it is to reject Platonism by the front door, only to re-admit it by the rear. In later years Borges revealingly confessed that he was unfair to Plato in his earlier work, notably in *La historia de la eternidad:* the archetypes, he insists later, should be thought of as an everlasting *and* living reality (Burgin, 11-12).

III

The opposition between nature and convention is transformed in the Middle Ages into the dichotomy of realism/nominalism. Borges is fond of referring to Coleridge's view of men as either Aristotelians or Platonists:

> Los últimos sienten que las clases, los órdenes y los géneros son realidades; los primeros, que son generalizaciones; para éstos, el lenguaje no es otra cosa que un aproximativo juego de símbolos: para aquéllos es el mapa del universo. El platónico sabe que el universo es de algún modo un cosmos, un orden; ese orden, para el aristotélico, puede ser un error o una ficción de nuestro conocimiento parcial. (OI, 167-8)

While Borges found extravagant the claim by George Henry Lewis to the effect that the realist/nominalist debate was the only medieval issue of any importance, he certainly agreed with the significance that Lewis, by implication, attached to this philosophical dichotomy. As he explains: "La historia de la filosofía, no es un vano museo de distracciones y de juegos verbales; verosímilmente, las dos tesis corresponden a dos maneras de intuir la realidad" (OI, 214). Thus Plato is followed by Spinoza, Kant, and Francis Bradley, and Aristotle, by Locke, Hume, and William James. Naturally, we are eager to know with which group Borges sees himself as aligned.[9]

The realist argues that human potential is most fulfilled when the individual sheds what is peculiar to himself: "anhela con extraño amor los quietos arquetipos de las criaturas" (HE, 34). An extreme realism, which holds that reality is accessible only to those able to raise themselves out of the body, found support in the conservative elements of the Church and in the feudal nobility. It was challenged increasingly throughout the Middle Ages. The "moderate realism" of Thomism was itself symptomatic of major social change, whereby an urban bourgeoisie, pressing the claims of "reason" and secular law, destabilized the traditional dominance of the rural aristocracy.[10] In turn this moderate realism is attacked by the nominalist who "niega la verdad de los arquetipos y quiere congregar en un segundo los detalles del universo" (HE, 34). This applies not merely to the notion of Platonic universals as existing independently of the mind but even as the mind's own creations. In other words nominalism marks a decisive stage in the passage from symbol to sign that takes place in the discourse of the Middle Ages.[11] Attention became focused not upon universal mental representations but upon the unicity of the thing, isolated from any transcendental setting.

Nominalism exerted a profound influence on the fifteenth-century Terminist movement, which privileges the "term" (i.e., sign) at the expense of the concept (i.e., symbol). The effect of such emphasis is to enhance the status of the Arts, as an independent faculty within the Academy. More generally, the reduction of reality to a combination of terms naturally redounded to the benefit of the novel, whose development as a genre is closely involved with the rising fortunes of nominalism.

Despite an attempted shift towards the concrete, however, the Terminists were themselves guilty of over-refinement in their use of language as a medium for expressing complex ideas, which, in turn, invited criticism from a humanist movement, one of whose chief

---

[9] Compare Borges' comment in *Prólogos:* "Imaginar que en la etimología se cifran ocultas y preciosas verdades es notoriamente un error, ya que las palabras son símbolos casuales e inconstantes" (167).

[10] See Goldmann, 26.

[11] See Kristeva, "From Symbol to Sign" (1986), 62-73.

claims to originality lay in the importance that it attached to the genuine contextualization of discourse. The humanist rhetoricians furthered the nominalist subversion of philosophical verbiage by arguing the need to escape the excessively abstract terminology of scholasticism and to return to the reality of the *res*. Thus, nominalism, defined as a philosophical attitude, rather than as a rigorously defined epistemological standpoint, continued to colour their writing as it had that of the Terminists.[12]

Whereas the Terminist system was elitist, serving only a small group of clerics, humanism appealed to the merchants and bankers who constituted the new, rising bourgeoisie. With the triumph of this class in the modern world, nominalism, as Borges himself notes, has assumed all the force of an instinct: "Ahora, semejantes al espontáneo y alelado prosista de la comedia, todos hacemos nominalismo *sans le savoir:* es como una premisa general de nuestro pensamiento, un axioma adquirido" (HE, 34). Victory came not merely through force of arms, but also through political alliance. The bourgeoisie, while challenging the feudal aristocracy, at the same time marries into it. After all, it supports and fosters revolutions historically only to the extent that it covets the privileges, prestige, and wealth of the aristocracy. Intellectually, it is prepared to make comparable compromises: Plato, less familiar than Aristotle to the Middle Ages, is quietly reinstated. The realm of Platonic Ideals, whatever its shortcomings, offered the possibility of an escape from the world of time and chance, to which the nominalist view, in contrast, seemed irredeemably attached: "Los arquetipos y la eternidad – dos palabras – prometen posesiones más firmes. Lo cierto es que la sucesión es una intolerable miseria y que los apetitos magnánimos codician todos los minutos del tiempo y toda la variedad del espacio" (HE, 35). And so, philosophical realism continues to survive, although banished to the margins of the text or playfully inserted into its body:

> El nominalismo, antes la novedad de unos pocos, hoy abarca a toda la gente; su victoria es tan vasta y fundamental que su nombre es inútil. Nadie se declara nominalista porque no hay quien sea otra cosa. Tratemos de entender, sin embargo, que para los hombres de la Edad Media lo sustantivo no eran los hombres

---

[12] See Read (1983), 56-60, 100.

> sino la humanidad, no los individuos sino la especie, no las especies sino el género, no los géneros sino Dios. (OI, 214-15)

This residual realism is a bridge across which Borges will pass into his fictions. Let us illustrate this point by reference to "Deutches Requiem":

> Se ha dicho que todos los hombres nacen aristotélicos o platónicos. Ello equivale a declarar que no hay debate de carácter abstracto que no sea un momento de la polémica de Aristóteles y Platón; a través de los siglos y latitudes, cambian los nombres, los dialectos, las caras, pero no los eternos antagonistas. (A, 90-91)

Zur Linde is the Platonist who raises everthing to the category of symbol, and then categorizes the symbols *sub specie aeternitatis*. To so order the world is, needless to say, to dematerialize it, in such a way as to demonstrate unambiguously the Platonist's idealist affiliations: "Aseveran los teólogos que si la atención del Señor se desviara un solo segundo de mi derecha mano que escribe, ésta recaería en la nada" (86). David Jerusalem, the poet and unrepentant particularist, is the Aristotelian. Whereas Zur Linde raises the universe to the level of cold, disembodied abstraction, Jerusalem "se alegra de cada cosa, con minucioso amor. No comete jamás enumeraciones, catálogos" (88). The result is a corpus of poetry exhibiting proximity to the real, steeped in magical life and vitality. For the author of such a corpus, the most exquisite form of torture is not physical imprisonment but mental confinement to a world of reified universals. Suicide is Jerusalem's only means of escape from the map of Hungary, of which Zur Linde, with all the acumen of the true sadist, has obliged him to think constantly. He is the scapegoat that bears away all the sins of civilized man, the flesh that the idealist puts to death in order to defend the symbolic order.[13]

---

[13] As Anton Ehrenzweig writes: "The more strongly the Germans entertained heroic fantasies of self-destruction and a Wagnerian twilight of the gods, the more were they compelled to project their fears on devil-like figures, international conspiracies and cunning subversion, fears that at last concentrated on Jewish minorities, which somehow had always served as scapegoats to relieve internal social tension within their host societies. As marginal members they had to be cast out or burned in order to save the body social. In this sense there is below the schizoid-oral level of Anti-Semitism also a depressive anal level of fantasy. There seems

Borges' allegiance to the realist mode is confirmed, in fictional terms, by his utilization of the symbol as opposed to the sign. The symbol, as Kristeva explains, is anti-paradoxical: in terms of its logic, two opposing units are mutually exclusive (Kristeva [1986], 65). Borges' protagonists constitute a contradiction whose appearance initiates the story, whose opposition sustains it, and whose resolution concludes it. The symbol stands opposed to the sign's "strained ambivalence," and to its capacity to encompass identity, similarity *and* disparity. Insofar as this complexity is indispensable to psychology, Borges does not, and cannot, create "personalities."

However, since for the idealist all agonic conflicts are contained logically within his own fissured psyche, he must in the last instance break with the law of non-conjunction. Realism and nominalism inhabit the recesses of his own being. The attraction of the Other comes both from without and from within. It is another land, but one most intimate. Thus does Zur Linde discern in the poet "el símbolo de Una detestada zona de mi alma" (A, 89). The split, divided subject confronts himself: "Yo agonicé con él, yo morí con él, yo de algún modo me he perdido con él."

IV

The agonic conflict of the kind that Borges explored in his fiction is played out upon a cosmic scale. Freud, following Goethe, saw the necessity for this. For while a strong egoism protects an individual (be he man or god) from psychic disintegration, "in the last resort we must begin to love in order not to fall ill" (Freud, XI, 78). And if the Almighty is love, he must perforce "flow over" into his Creation, and become incarnate in a creature made in His own image: "Si en Dios están todas las cosas, todas las cosas estarán en el hombre, que es su reflejo terrenal" (P, 161). But if God needs an adoring "other" to receive and, equally importantly, to return, his love, the opposition remains unequal, since ultimately everything must be an emanation from God. So at least argue the Gnostics, in

---

something in the Jewish fate which symbolizes an anal fantasy of voluntarily casting oneself out" (Ehrenzweig, 258).

Edna Aizenberg's interpretation of "Deutsches Requiem" is diametrically opposed to my own. She sees the story as celebrating the Jewish "mind" and "intellect" (see Aizenberg, 129-30).

whose eyes the world is degraded by its sheer contingency (D, 65) and mankind by its derivative status vis-à-vis the archetypal Adam Kadman (SN, 133).

The Gnostics, as Borges explains, influenced the Cabbalists. Both assume the notion of the Great Chain of Being, which accords to each created thing a specific position in a creation hierarchically conceived. This notion is conducive to a doctrine of correspondence, whose affinity with Cabbalism, Borges suggests, has been neglected (P, 161), and which relates to one of his favourite subjects, mirrors. In his context Borges rejects the classical defence of evil, which sees evil simply in specular terms, as the negative image of good. *Desdicha,* Borges insists, is not an absence of *dicha,* but is (felt as) something positive. Leibniz, he continues, saw evil as necessary for the variety of the world, as necessary as the dark patches are to the light in a Rembrandt canvas (SN, 135). In the same way, hell is the other, necessary face of Heaven: "Su reverso preciso es necesario para el equilibrio de la Creación" (P. 158).

The concept of the Chain of Being is sustained by a criterion of *simplicity* an understanding of which is crucial to the correct appreciation of Borges' own treatment of Gnostic and Cabbalistic themes. Mazzeo is enlightening in this respect: "Each higher being on the ladder possesses a greater degree of all the potentialities of living beings, a greater capacity to perform more of the functions and activities that life is capable of, from eating to thinking. However, the higher beings are really characterized not by complexity but by a great unity and simplicity, according to this way of thought" (Mazzeo, 173). The basic division is between the body and soul. The less body that an entity possesses, the more it partakes of the Ideal. Man himself is a microcosm, the *vinculum mundi,* who mirrors within himself the larger cosmic design. In him the battle against the flesh assumes macro proportions.

In "Tres versiones de Judas," Borges explored a paradoxical version of cosmic reflexion, by seeing the Devil as Christ's mirror image, and, ultimately, as identical with Him. This story is particularly interesting since it reveals, albeit tangentially, the importance for language of the criterion of contingency: "Quienes recorran este artículo, deben asimismo considerar que no registra sino las conclusiones de Runeberg, no su dialéctica y sus pruebas" (F, 176). Here, Borges graphically avoids *weighing down* his own fictional constructs with irrelevant *matter.* The briefer a story the better, in his view. Indeed, what the writer offers are not so much stories as plot summaries of another writer's stories, so that, after the manner of the Sacred Texts, his own narrative is cleansed of all redundancy: "Suponer un error en la Escritura es intolerable; no menos intolerable es admitir un hecho casual en el más precioso acontecimiento de la historia del mundo" (177).

And yet meaning is elusive. Cleansed of obfuscating redundancy, all elements of the text are over-determined. This very semantic density reproduces problems of interpretation, although at a higher level. The onus falls upon the interpreter to restore an absolute primal discourse which commentary, by its very nature, can never express. Words proliferate in the hermeneutic struggle, in which commentary succumbs to the pull of material inertia.

In the same way does the textual body of the world elude our grasp. Nature is a book that one opens and pores over, whose signs one ponders, but whose meaning flickers darkly "because the similitudes that form the graphics of the world are one 'cog' out of alignment with those that form its discourse" (Foucault [1970], 30). Just as the Bible consisted of a series of fables, hiding a mystical truth, so the world was structured as a series of heavens, through which we pass on our journey to the god-head: our open sesame is the Name of the Father. We seek a god who "carece majestuosamente de nombre" (D, 62).

Borges' "Los teólogos" constitutes his most extensive fictional treatment of the theme of cosmic reflection. Aureliano and Juan de Panonia are caught, in typically Borgesian manner, in an agonic conflict. The violence that exists between them is born not merely of their differences but also of their similarities: "Militaban los dos en el mismo ejército, anhelaban el mismo galardón, guerreaban contra el mismo Enemigo, pero Aureliano no escribió una palabra que inconfesablemente no propendiera a superar a Juan" (A, 41). In other words, each is the mirror image of the other. The art of tragedy, René Girard has warned, is based on such specular dichotomies: twins are matching images of violence (Girard, 70-73).

The dialogue between the two theologians is destined to be tragic for the simple reason that they both want the same thing: scholastic pre-eminence within their chosen field of specialization, heresy. Parents may be excused for believing that the actual object of sibling rivalry is irrelevant, in the sense that each child seems merely to covet what the other possesses. If however we are prepared, with the psychoanalyst, to delve beneath the surface skirmishes, we will discover that all such rivalry ultimately converges on the one object of desire, namely the phallus, symbol of total presence and means of union with Mother. Aureliano and Juan battle, like rival brothers, over the right to fire, the phallic symbol of godly power, which Prometheus snatched from the parent-god. Juan is more generously endowed; his success rests upon the sizeable *body* of his singularly exhaustive text. His refutations inflict upon Aureliano a symbolic castration. He thereby sets the terms of battle for his colleague, who decides to anticipate Juan on a subsequent occasion: "quería superar a Juan de Panonia para curarse del rencor que éste le infundía, no para hacerle mal" (A, 39).

But Aureliano has miscalculated. The genital stage is superimposed upon the anal stage, whose influence continues to be felt. In a sudden shift in evaluative criteria, the sources and references of his subsequent scholarly treatise are transformed into the dead weight of the body, the tradition behind a text, which accords patriarchal primacy to predecessors. Juan's version represents a superior truth in terms of economy: "Era irrisoriamente breve, [. . .] límpido, universal; no parecía redactado por una persona concreta, sino por cualquier hombre o, quizá, por todos los hombres" (40-41). His text has assumed the status of a Platonic ideal. The realization of what has happened comes slowly to Aureliano; he looks on Juan's treatise with disdain, and then with fear, as he understands that yet again he has been eclipsed. The spirit has triumphed over the body: "Aureliano sintió una humillación física" (41).

Dialogue is a tragic, fateful confrontation between two protagonists who are evenly matched, indeed, who are reflections of the same archetype: "lo que hay abajo es igual a lo que hay arriba, y lo que hay arriba, igual a lo que hay abajo; en el Zohar, [. . .] el mundo inferior es reflejo del superior'" (43). The resemblance between the combatants grows until they become doubles. The more the conflict is prolonged, the more we sense that its outcome will be violent. To spare an enemy brother from death or exile is to condemn oneself to such a fate.

But at the same time, in the case of any doubles, there is never anything on one side of an opposition that cannot be found on the other side, provided that we wait long enough:[14] as Aureliano sum-

---

[14] See Girard, 158.

marizes an heretical doctrine with a short prayer that suddenly came to him, he suspects another source, which he subsequently traces to the writings of Juan. By condemning Juan, therefore, he condemns himself, or rather abjects that (material) part of himself that threatens his own (spiritual) identity. Without the break (comparable to the thetic break), he cannot be, yet at Juan's execution he witnesses his own. The hater and the hated are, for God, the same person. For what shines through both, when they transcend their individualities, is nothing other than the image of God.

It is at this very moment, however, when Borges projects his work onto the cosmic level of myth that it is important to read him against the grain. From such resistance is born the realization that what is played out in "Los teólogos" relates less to medieval hermeneutics than to the idealist narrative of the moving Spirit, that breaks with identity only to recuperate it narcissistically at a higher level. Understood in this way, the cabbalistic exegete reveals himself to be a bourgeois subject that "requires some Other to assure itself that its powers and properties are more than hallucinatory, that its activities have meaning because they take place in a shared objective world; yet such otherness is also intolerable to the subject and must be expelled or introjected" (Eagleton [1990], 71). Here lies the truth of the claim that we create our own predecessors.

V

More liberal critics have sought to underplay Borges' attachment to the world of the epic. Sturrock, for example, writes: "I cannot believe that Borges's fictions are born of humiliation, or of a genuine nostalgia for the bravery of those ancestors who went to war in South America in the epic days of the nineteenth century" (Sturrock, 196). On this occasion, we cannot help but share the affront of other critics when faced with such a cavalier dismissal of what Borges has so roundly stated himself: "Nunca he dejado de sentir nostalgia de ese destino épico que las divinidades me negaron, sin duda sabiamente. La poesía comienza por la poesía épica; su primer tema fue la guerra" (Barnatán, 30). Of course, intentions, as we know, are nothing unless realized in the text. In this case, however, evidential support is not lacking: Borges' work reveals a profound, insidious attraction for the epic hero, as embodied in Rosas and Perón, "the exact counterpart of his own meditative self" (Rodríguez Monegal [1971], 21).[15] The bookish Borges has confessed again and again to the sense of not having lived enough, a sense vividly brought home by the epic hero, whose life is all action.

Such confessions notwithstanding, the epic appeals to him not by virtue of its proximity to life, but, conversely, by its literary distance from life. To this extent there is some truth to Sturrock's claim. Borges is dismissive of traditional attempts to elide the epic with nature: both old epics, like the *Cid,* and modern epics, such as *Martín Fierro,* do not in his view aspire to mimetic realism.[16] Their realism is strictly of a philosophical ilk. Gaucho poetry is "tan artificial como cualquier otro [género]" (D, 153). Effective though the *Iliad, Beowulf,* and the *Chanson de Roland* are, "todos, sin embargo, adolecen del pecado original de lo literario; son estructuras, formas hechas de símbolos" (EC, 148).

Borges' comments undoubtedly spring from a central valid insight, that the epic pursues the general through the specific. Its preferred linguistic mode is that of metaphoric similarity as distinct from metonymic contiguity. Beneath the narrative flux of the *Cid,* which seems to favour the syntagmatic axis, the organizing principle is that of paradigmatic hierarchization. The result is a fundamentally theological perspective on the world, and an absolute conviction in the literal sense of the word.

The epic system is ruled by the symbol, which preserves, albeit in an idealized form, a rudimentary, magical belief in a primary link between signifier and signified. As Kristeva comments: "[Symbols] refer back to one or more unknowable and unrepresentable universal transcendence(s); univocal connections link the transcendences to the units evoking them" (Kristeva [1986], 64). Thus, for example, the Cid embodies the qualities of heroism and courage; the King, of justice and reason; and the Infantes, of fear and treason. From the beginning, good and evil are locked in mortal combat,

---

[15] Borges gives fictional expression in "El Sur" to his personal nostalgia for the military, heroic tradition of his family, which played no part in his own life.

[16] Borges quotes an example of the naturalist view: "Tanto valiera repudiar el arrullo de la paloma porque no es un madrigal, o la canción del viento porque no es una oda. Así esta pintoresca payada se ha de considerar en la rusticidad de su forma y en la ingenuidad de su fondo como una voz elemental de la naturaleza" (D, 31-32).

with each clearly and unambiguously defined, showing no compromise.

One consequence of this transcendental elevation is the absence of individual personality. The epic subject is real to the extent that he imitates or repeats an archetype. The plot of which he is a function, whilst it comprises historical events, unfolds as a totality within the timelessness of myth. The attraction of this primitive ontology to such an author as Borges is obvious: it privileges event over character and discourages the investigation of characters' psychic states.[17] At the same time, the lure elicits an act of misrecognition. The idealist mistakes his own crisis of identity in a post-capitalist age for the lack of individuation in the pre-capitalist organic community. In other words he discerns in medieval collectivism a mirror image of the subjective flux which he experiences in the privacy of his own being. Even the authorial anonymity of the epic bard reminds him of the problematic status of his own author(ity): "Like the epic poet, [. . .] Borges also 'knows that his song is not his alone'" (Christ, 31). Naturally, Borges approves of epic formulae, such as the Kenningar, which transformed the whole of Norse literature into an autonomous, corporate enterprise, and which he equates with the public metaphors of his own classical idiom (HE, 43-68).

But however undeniable the similarities, the fact remains that they stem from a fundamental misprision. If in medieval society individuals coincide with themselves, it is because they are still innocent of what a later bourgeois age will mistakenly take to be a primary rupture, between the public and the private selves. In medieval culture, only those emotions that are exteriorized exist. The hero in particular is an integral personality, without a mask and therefore unable to be unmasked. Mature reflection reveals that the intimate, feminine world of the idealist is far removed from the hierarchized world of feudalism, in which identity coincides absolutely with social being. The epic subject, on this evidence, is the transcendental ego, knowing only pure consciousness. His patronymic encapsulates his very essence: both are sometimes called into question, but never radically so. His social world is turbulent, but fundamentally unproblematic. The laws of chivalry hold the aggressivity of the id firmly in check.

---

[17] See Christ, 31.

One important fact is emerging: if Borges correctly intuited certain fundamental aspects of the epic, he did not press his intuitions to the point at which they exhibit the genre's (and his own) firmly entrenched class bias. This bias is evinced principally by the fact that the epic has been cleansed of all plebeian matter. The realm of the "Fathers" holds itself aloof from the world of ordinary men and women.[18] We, who inhabit this world, look on, and upwards, from afar; our fate is to marvel reverentially at the hero's courtly splendour. And, as might any politically dominant class, the feudal aristocracy projects this splendour as "natural" and eternal. For this reason the epic exists in an absolute past. It knows perpetual movement, but lies outside of history. The narrative describes a self-enclosed cycle, whose final outcome exists *in potentia* at the beginning, "since the function of the symbol [. . .] exists prior to the actual symbolic statement" (Kristeva [1986], 65). Its movement, however dynamic, is tangential to the present. Events unfold *sub specie aeternitatis,* in accordance with an all-pervasive Platonism.

Similarly, the language of the epic is a class language, blissfully unaware of its own boundaries, uninhibited by the desire of the Other. It knows no diglossia, accommodates no alien ways; the hero's discourse merges with the author's, which merges with the community's, on the basis of a prevailing belief system.[19] Dialogue, genuine or otherwise, is largely precluded.

VI

"No creo que sea un autor muy importante" (Sorrentino, 29). With this single, curt statement, Borges excludes from his predecessors a writer, Juan Ruiz, author of the *Libro de buen amor* (1330, 1343), who presides over the key transition in the thirteenth and fourteenth centuries from the symbol to the sign. That Borges was drawn more to symbolic practice is beyond question, a fact which would in itself account for his negative reaction to the *Libro.* The latter's moralizing passages, in their symbolic assurance, are literally split off from the carnival body of the text, which subjects all pre-

---

[18] See Bakhtin (1981), 15.
[19] See Bakhtin (1981), 334-5. For further treatment of the theme of language in the *Cid,* see Read (1983), chapter 1.

tence to univocal, legitimate meaning to the ravages of parody and satire. Since he himself belonged to a class, the decadent bourgeoisie, whose authority was being questioned, Borges necessarily responded anxiously and dismissively to such a subversive, *bodily* text as the *Libro*. His own sympathies lie, as we have seen, with the epic, an aristocratic genre.

As a member of the bourgeoisie, however, even in its reactionary phase, Borges' actual relationship to such an over-determined text as the *Libro* can be nothing if not complex. He certainly recognised the significance of Chaucer, the Archpriest's eminent, and in many ways comparable, contemporary, within the development from allegory to the novel, a development which he correctly understood to be part of the broader philosophical shift from realism to nominalism (OI, 215). Nominalism was to be an indispensable ingredient in modernist art, as practised by the author of the *Ficciones*, particularly through its insistence on the arbitrary nature of the sign. It feeds directly into such ideological categories as "liberty" and the "open society," which facilitate and protect the operations of the market economy. In their different ways, both Juan Ruiz and Borges luxuriate in the freedom that nominalistic conventionalism confers.

It is not merely bourgeois progressivism whose effects Borges registers but also the insecurity which is its converse. The *Libro* gives the appearance of having capsized, so as to produce a fragmented, linear structure, which at no point connects with any transcendental dimension. What Gabriel Josipovici says of Chaucer is true of Juan Ruiz: "he no longer seems to have faith in the essential meaningfulness of the universe created by God" (Josipovici, 102). The sheer proliferation of "authorities" to support points of view completely neutralizes the whole concept of Authority: "decoration becomes frenzied to keep from the artist's mind the fact that it is decoration round a hollow, an emptiness, a silence" (103).[20] Without such predecessors as Chaucer and Juan Ruiz, Borges' philosophical scepticism, his monadic isolation verging on solipsism, would be unthinkable.

Yet, finally, Borges' intuitive rejection of Juan Ruiz deserves respectful consideration since it was, in its own terms, substantially valid. The Archpriest, it is true, exhibits the kind of organicist nos-

---

[20] For more detail, see Read (1983), chapter 2.

talgia that should have appealed to Borges. His work gives ample evidence of the alienation which was to characterize in grosser terms the fully-fledged bourgeois society. Only in such a society is value projected abstractly as money ("Don Dinero") and love as an immaterial, generalized Desire ("Buen Amor"). Even words assume, in their conventionality, the status of mere tokens: if the unity of the signal is relinquished by Juan Ruiz for a variable range of localized meanings, this range corresponds, within a social context, to an endless variety of situations, whose effect is to make dialogue impossible. Despite his reservations concerning the new order, however, Juan Ruiz has in his sights an aristocratic culture which an aspirant middle class was intent upon over-turning.[21] Borges, in contrast, is a modernist writer for whom, in the absence of a genuinely revolutionary philosophy, a critique of modern (bourgeois) civilization can only assume the trappings of an aristocratic elitism.

It is in these terms that we should understand the points of both convergence and divergence between Borges and Juan Ruiz. Superficially, the resemblances are close. Compare, for example, the opposition that Juan Ruiz establishes between his person(a) and his protagonist as *alter ego* with the dichotomy that Borges creates between himself and the "other" Borges. Significantly, both writers are eager to surrender their author(ity) to the Reader and a collective Tradition, in a manner which confirms their common origins in pre- or early capitalist society and contrasts starkly with the behaviour of the aggressive, autonomous subject of subsequent capitalist formations. At the same time, however, any such perceived resemblance between the two writers involves a kind of misprision. Juan Ruiz's subject fragments under the pressure of bodily drives. "A carnival participant is both actor and spectator; he loses his sense of individuality, passes through a zero point of carnivalesque activity and splits into a subject of the spectacle and an object of the game" (Kristeva [1980], 78).[22] Through this subject, Juan Ruiz is able to estrange the ideology of the crumbling feudal order from within. In contrast, Borges' passive, decentred subject, abstracted from all time and space, is the index not simply of a primitive mode of capitalist production but of colonial marginalization with indus-

---

[21] See Rodríguez Puértolas (1976), 71-103.
[22] For the classic treatment of the carnivalization of literature, see Bakhtin (1968).

trial capitalism. Liberation from the Oedipal constraints of a dominant culture occurs in a desperately backward society, whose indigenous culture had been expunged by imperialist European powers. In this situation, individual identity is an idealist creation, whose bodily drives are rigorously sublimated and recontained, in a politically conservative manner, within the unity of consciousness. Disruptive of traditional values, it is yet complicit with the world of international capitalist production. And it is to the process of its historical formation that we must now turn.

CHAPTER II

PUBLIC USAGE AND PRIVATE ABUSAGE
IN THE AGE OF CONFLICT

I

No other work better captures the crisis of the fourteenth century, which preludes the disintegration of the medieval world, than does Juan Manuel's *El Conde Lucanor* (1335). The author's attempt to protect his manuscripts against scribal corruption, which led him to place safe copies in the Monastery of Peñafiel (Manuel, 68), indicates a concern with property rights which both registers the insecurity of a noble class increasingly threatened by radical changes corroding the feudal system and anticipates the possessiveness that was to characterize the new capitalist mode of production. Insofar as Juan Manuel himself plundered popular tradition for his stories, we can hardly blame Borges for ignoring copy-right considerations and recasting one of them, "El brujo postergado," in his *Historia universal de la infamia*.

Doubtless Borges was encouraged by the fact that Juan Manuel's collection of stories exhibits the kind of framing devices and author/narrator problematic that typify the new genre of the *fabliella*. It was not, however, to such devices that Borges was in the present case attracted, but to a story which allowed him to drammatize internally, as it were, the whole opposition between literature and life, or, to be more precise, to allegorize the act of reading and writing in terms of betrayal.[1] In this story a dean retires into Don Illán's study – in both the sense of a room apart and his books – to learn the art of magic (or of fiction?). After reneging on promises to pro-

---

[1] See Sturrock, 34-36. For a detailed comparison of Don Juan Manuel's original story and Borges' recasting, see Montgomery.

mote Don Illán's affairs, the dean suddenly finds himself returned (from literature) to life, and to the real circumstances that preceded his entry into illusion (HI, 119-23).

It is perilously tempting to follow Borges himself in seeing this story as just one more chapter in a *universal* history, and thereby to misrecognise one of his predecessors. But we are reminded, through further reflection, that Juan Manuel wrote for an aristocratic audience, anxious to know and so to defend itself against a reality which aroused in it a sense of suspicion and insecurity. Fidelity and loyalty figure prominently in the system of feudal relations, and in a world in which these relations were increasingly at risk, Juan Manuel felt it opportune to offer corporative support to his class.[2] Into this alien context Borges projects (and in the process disguises) the egoistic individualism and mutual indifference that characterize the historically localized monads of (monopoly) capitalism. As Jean Franco rightly (and brilliantly) argues, the specific context of Borges' own obsession is the classic dilemma of the free-floating intellectual: having betrayed his patriarchal, bourgeois masters (oedipally, his parents) and abandoned his fellow artists, along with the masses whose revolutionary interests the avant-garde sometimes aspired to serve, Borges finds himself burdened with the guilt of his private indulgence in literature.[3] For Juan Manuel, such guilt could never arise, if only because it involves from his perspective the anachronistic division between public and private.

II

The effects of the division of labour in a slavery-based Greek society were mitigated up to a point by the substantial unity between the people and the State and the consequent absence of any separation of the private and public spheres. In medieval times there was, if possible, an even less clear-cut opposition between State and society, between political and economic life. Civil society was political society to the extent that socio-economic distinctions (serf and lord) were also political distinctions (subject and sovereign). An in-

---

[2] See Blanco Aguinaga *et al.*, I, 122. For a good socio-political perspective on Don Juan Manuel, see Rodríguez-Puértolas, 45-69.

[3] See Franco, 60; and also Jameson (1981), 258n43.

dividual was defined in terms of his estate, and his behaviour governed by specific vital norms. Moreover, since medieval culture discouraged individuation, people were never in doubt as to their own identity.[4]

The absence of an interior/exterior dichotomy corresponds, in medieval society, with a considerable degree of collective psychic unity. While the soul is never directly joined to the body, just as an abyss separates the divine and the worldly, it certainly informs the body. This explains why, necessarily, a beautiful soul is reflected in a beautiful body, and why the sinner is a physical monstrosity. The body is needed to "save appearances," for it is through these appearances that we are able to read the sacred signs of God. It is for this reason that, as we argued above, the "substantial forms" of feudal organicism cannot suppose the existence of an inner as opposed to an outer realm, and that people were either serf or master, and, within these broad categories, nobles, vassals, serfs, sinners, or the faithful.[5]

Clearly, if there can be no isolated soul, there can be no individual subject as such:

> The low degree of sublimation, corresponding to the low level of technology, means [. . .] a weaker ego, an ego which has not yet come to terms (by negation) with the pregenital impulses of its own body. But the pregenital impulses are there. The result is that the pregenital impulses, all the fantastic wishes of infantile narcissism, express themselves in unsublimated form, so that archaic man retains the magic body of infancy.
> Hence archaic man characteristically has a massive structure of excremental magic, which indicates the bodily fantasies from which the disembodied fantasies of sublimation are derived. (Brown [1968], 261)

One consequence of this is that we are able to observe the repressed fantasies of capitalism in their sublimated forms: "The monetary system itself of the European Middle Ages retained archaistic memories of the true worth of money" (261).

---

[4] See Marx, *Critique of Hegel's Doctrine of the State,* in *Early Writings,* 57-198 (90); and Ruitenbeek, 36.

[5] See Rodríguez, 96-98, 204-6. It would be difficult to overestimate my debt to this masterly work, particularly in the present chapter.

While remaining within the feudal matrix, a number of marginal religious movements of the low Middle Ages, along with such diverse phenomena as witchcraft, astrology, and various kinds of magic, emphasized the "living" spirit of things, as opposed to their corporeality. Perhaps the most significant of these movements was Cabbalism. Not surprisingly, in view of his attraction to the naturalist thesis, Borges was deeply attached to a Cabbalistic tradition which transposed the whole Platonic, Cratylean myth into Christian terms:

> Adán y las estrellas lo supieron
> En el Jardín. La herrumbre del pecado
> (Dicen los cabalistas) lo ha borrado
> Y las generaciones lo perdieron. (OP, 147)

As we saw earlier, the corporeal aspects of Platonism are residual. Ultimately, its forms are trenchantly idealistic: the ethereal world of Ideas is a dream world, arrived at through a process of sublimation. Deeply indebted to Platonism, Cabbalism also relinquishes the sensible for the spiritual, the visible for the invisible. How and why is its materialism jettisoned? In its original, God-given form, language displayed a close, unambiguous relationship with or resemblance to things. However, its transparent form was clouded at Babel by an infusion of matter. And to the extent that language resides in the world, the world as a book resists our understanding. As Borges explains: "[. . .] el mundo externo –las formas, las temperaturas, la luna– es un lenguaje que hemos olvidado los hombres, o que deletreamos apenas" (OI, 171).

To begin to make sense of the scrambled text that confronts him when he gazes upon the world, the reader depends upon the secondary discourse of the commentary. The task of commentary is to restore that primal text beneath the surface of language. The interpreter aims to cleanse this language of its detritus, which, to take Borges' own example, clogs up the reports of a robbery as it appears in our newspapers. In journalism it is the length and sound of the paragraphs, in other words, the actual forms of language, that constitute the intrusive material element. In poetry, on the other hand, it is the contingency of the content of discourse which, according to Borges, symptomizes our post-Babelian misery (D, 58-59).

The model of the perfect textual body, of course, is the Bible, regarding which "el vago concepto de azar ningún sentido tiene" (D, 59). However chaotic its surface forms may be, we can be sure that the sacred scripture is ultimately devoid of all redundancy:

> Imaginemos ahora esa inteligencia estelar, dedicada a manifestarse, no en dinastías ni en aniquilaciones ni en pájaros, sino en voces escritas. Imaginemos asimismo, de acuerdo con la teoría pre-agustiniana de inspiración verbal, que Dios dicta, palabra por palabra lo que se propone decir. Esa premisa (que fue la que asumieron los cabalistas) hace de la Escritura un texto absoluto, donde la colaboración del azar es calculable en cero. (D, 59)

In exemplary fashion, the Scriptures are impenetrable to contingency; revelations lie in wait behind their most insignificant detail and man is bound to sit and interrogate them "hasta lo absurdo" (D, 60).

The Cabbalist tradition, strong in Spain despite the expulsion of the Jews, subsequently spread (with this expulsion) to the rest of Europe, and continued to exert fascination in the seventeenth century.[6] And wherever it spread, however mechanical its practice, it encouraged exegetists not to rest in one simple, solid, constant meaning. Mystical hermeneutics took root particularly in Germany, where it was used by Protestant reformers to foster the notion of the divine power of the German language, on the basis of which scholars were able to defend its use as the vehicle of the Scriptures. German appeared alongside Hebrew as a prospective Adamic language.[7]

During the course of these developments, certain tensions and contradictions within these mystical movements emerged more clearly. The Cabbalist exhibits all the characteristics of a Platonic view of language which, in its Cratylean mode, presupposes a residual magical belief in the power of the word. The word is not an arbitrary token within an insubstantial system: it exists as part of the natural world, a material object among other such objects. Foucault has noted how even Ramus, for all his apparent modernity, was drawn not to the "meaning" of language, but to the intrinsic "prop-

---

[6] See Swietlicki.
[7] See Padley (1985), 87-89.

erties" of letters, syllables, and finally words (Foucault [1970], 35).[8] Within the private realm in which the mystic operates, the body is transfigured by its association with the spirit, and it is to this body reborn that the mystic will return. Regression occurs, through textual analysis, to the origins of Christianity. And of course, since in the end all origins are in the Body, modern advocates of the virtues of the pleasure-principle have found in the likes of Jacob Boehme forceful exponents of "die sensualische Sprache." For example, Norman O. Brown writes: "It is the language appropriate to a species that is actualizing the true potentialities of its sensuous nature and all life" (Brown [1968], 72). Even when he talks of the spirit, it is to the body that the mystic refers: "[t]he dreamer awakes not from a body but to a body" (Brown [1966], 222).

Notwithstanding the causal affinity between word and thing, however, Platonism erects an intermediate realm of Ideas, between the forms of nature and those of language, and thereby cushions language against the impact of the material body. Under the pressure of sublimation, the feudal notion of society as organic passes into a spiritual variant, that of the mystic body, and the idea of the Church as a body into that of the spiritual body of the Church.[9]

Undoubtedly, German mysticism had very strong reasons to repress its material dimensions, connecting as these do with the birth of the modern revolutionary era, in the form of the Peasants' Revolt.[10] Such conservatism alerts us to the ambiguity of Cabbalism's textual *jouissance*. Hermeneutical practice opens a route to communion with the "mental" language of God. Its "deep secrets" were based on a rigid, static Chain of Being, ascent of which, along a vertical axis, marked a process of increasing spiritualization. The stability of this structure, which included the social hierarchy, was to be ensured at any cost. Linguistically, authority is exerted through grammars and textual criticism. Condemning the typographical method, Protestantism engages in the oppressive literalization of discourse, which brings to an end the Cabbalistic proliferation of meaning, in accordance with Ramus' atomistic view of language

---

[8] Foucault concludes: "The study of grammar in the sixteenth century is based upon the same epistemological arrangement as the science of nature or the esoteric disciplines."
[9] See Rodríguez, 59, 66-67.
[10] See Bronowski and Mazlish, 113.

and the nominalist belief that plain truth can be expressed without ornamentation.[11]

But of course, if this authoritarian binding of the linguistic body served a reactionary purpose, it could also be turned to a different account. In this sense, the contradictions of Lutheranism are profound. In intent a conservative rather than a progressive movement, it contributed largely, in practice, to the waves of change coursing through sixteenth-century Europe.

Luther himself hated the economic individualism of the age and attacked it fiercely in his pamphlets. But the result of his divorce of man's inner life from civic activity was to free economics from ethical and religious responsibilities. The literalization and spatialization of discourse preludes the "plain style" of science and a preoccupation with the virtues of contact with things. The body of language is bound so as to hoard the energy with which to fuel the bourgeois enterprise.

III

The Cabbalistic implications of Platonism's basis in idealism are most thoroughly explored in fictional terms by Borges in "La muerte y la brújula." The protagonists, Lönnrot and Red Scharlach, as their names indicate, are caught in a mirror relationship. One is the signifier and the other the signified. They are bound together by a common identity: no gap has opened up between them. At the same time, by a strange paradox, their very sense of fullness is also the source of aggression. Each needs the other to recognise him, to which end each must dominate the other, in terms of "the constitutional aggressivity of the human being who must always win his place at the expense of the other" (Lemaire, 179).

If, however, the origin of human aggression lies in the mirror phase, the Oedipal overlay is of fundamental importance to its subsequent transformation. In "La muerte y la brújula," we move in a world which is no longer concerned merely with the primary registration of bodily fullness in the mirror image. Borges' choice of genre is here surely revealing. For the detective story is the prime

---

[11] Cf. Brown (1966), 191 ff.

example of the Oedipal situation: it is based on a crime that precedes the beginning of the story. At the very outset, we move from the full, imaginary world of the mirror stage into the empty symbolic world of language, in which individuals are driven by a radical sense of lack. As always we need to remain alert to political determinations: at the turn of the century, the emergence of the detective story as a favourite Modernist device corresponds with an attempt by the bourgeoisie to affirm its hegemony during a critical period of transition. Within its Oedipal structure the reader could indulge his grisly interest in killing in a civilized manner.

The estuary ("cuyas aguas tienen el color del desierto" [F, 148]) marks a bar, between the conscious and the unconscious, the semiotic and the symbolic. The story begins in a hotel, that quintessential symbol of impersonality, which inflicts upon Yarmolinsky ("hombre de barba y ojos grises" [148]) a radical lack of being. While the Oedipus is the source of recognition of the other and of the principle of equality, it also institutes the castration seme that involves the split between mind and body. In the process the benign face of the double, formerly the immortal soul that guaranteed immortality, is transformed into a life-threatening assailant.[12]

In the post-Oedipal situation, the Ego will fuse with truth only through the possession of the name of the Father, "es decir, el conocimiento inmediato de todas las cosas que serán y que son y que han sido" (150). Lönnrot and Red Scharlach are twin brothers battling over this phallic endowment; they both aspire to total union with the Creation. But in order to be everything one must relinquish all circumstantial, idiosyncratic attributes. Victory goes to the antagonist who most successfully surrenders his materiality, or, in the internecine strife, reduces his opponent to a purely bodily consciousness. Initially, Red Scharlach is the loser: "Nueve días y nueve noches agonicé [. . .] Llegué a abominar de mi cuerpo, llegué a sentir que dos ojos, dos manos, dos pulmones, son tan monstruosos como dos caras" (159). An anal level is overlain by the genital phase. Scharlach is caught in the body as in the bowels: "yo sentía

---

[12] Freud describes the transition thus: "Such ideas [regarding the soul's immortality] have sprung from the soul of unbounded self-love, from the primary narcissism which dominates the mind of the child and of primitive man. But when this stage has been surmounted, the 'double' reverses its aspect. From having been an assurance of immortality, it becomes the uncanny harbinger of death" ("The Uncanny," XIV, [335-76], 357).

que el mundo es un laberinto, del cual era imposible huir" (159), but is penetrated by Lönnrot's castrating bullet. His feminization is turned to good account; after nine days (months?) of labour, he gives birth to a superior fiction.

Lönnrot aspires to absolute status. He searches for the name of God with total passion, poring over learned Jewish texts, extracting each letter from the fateful series of crimes. But there is a price to be paid for such single-mindedness: "las meras circunstancias, la realidad [. . .], apenas le interesaban" (156). The phenomenon of the initial umbilical cut, Lönnrot's reaction confirms, is constantly repeated in the course of subjective experience. The original lost object is the mother's body, and the detective pursues it obsessively, in a process of constant transcendence, omitting from his calculations the indispensable relationship between the sign and its referent. In the process he surrenders all contact between fiction and reality.

To the extent that Treviranus believes in the textual quality of reality at all, he mistakenly equates fiction with mimetic realism. Accordingly (as Lönnrot explains), he believes in the contingent nature of the criminal's "story," accepts that "interviene copiosamente el azar" (149). In contrast, Lönnrot correctly discerns that the solution to the crimes forms part of a text that has been swept clean of all matter. His own fatal error, as a rationalist who is also something of a gambler, lies in treating the edge in the (card) table as the boundary to another world, and in accordingly failing to realize that "[e]l primer término de la serie [. . .] fue dado por el azar" (160). It is his own knowledge of this contingency that enables Scharlach to construct a fiction which surpasses Lönnrot's in its abstraction. His text is more ethereal, more archetypal in the Platonic sense, than the detective's, upon whom he in turn inflicts symbolic castration.

In sum, the modern cabbalist text shows itself to be ideologically complex. Fiction withdraws into a private space to preserve feminine, bodily qualities deemed redundant in the market economy, while simultaneously it aspires to the abstract, therefore masculine, status of a Platonic archetype. In this situation of over-determination, the hermeneutist seeks both to indulge his writerly erotism *and* to cleanse the text of ambiguity, drawing it closer, that is, to the clarity of the spoken word.

Such complexity can only be fully understood within its social context. For Mother/Matter is, in the last instance, the new industrial proletariat whose increasing militancy after 1890 so aroused the anxiety of the patriarchal oligarchy in Argentina. Resentment towards this class was not directed against the immigrants in general, who largely constituted it, but towards the Jews, whose presence in large numbers (after 1900) gave a radical colouring to what was in essence a situation of class conflict.[13] While he is drawn to Cabbalism as towards some telluric source of energy, however, Borges will enclose it within the safety of a fictional form that boasts its remoteness from the real. And so his idealism will remain in the end (as in the beginning) a profoundly political gesture.

IV

For justification of this subjective reading of "La muerte y la brújula" – if any justification is needed – we have only to look to history, which demonstrates the continuity between the Cabbala and the aesthetic, and between the latter and the category of the subject. The various forms of feudal animism, of which Cabbalism was one of the most notable, helped prepare the way for the establishment of the bourgeois matrix in its early mercantilist phase, and, coincidentally, of the notion of the subject. Elements of feudal organicism, particularly in their animist guise, are moulded to new circumstances: the courtly notion of virtue, in conjunction with the self-consciousness of the knight, becomes the privileged soul of Platonism, a soul which, in turn, signals the birth of the individual subject.[14]

The proto-subject or *alma bella* produced by the aspirant bourgeoisie is the basis of a new poetic discourse, originating in Petrarch and elaborated in Spain by Garcilaso and Boscán, without which all subsequent lyrical discourse, including Borges' own substantial body of poetry, is unthinkable. I use the word "body" advisedly: the aesthetic (hence "beautiful" soul) initiates the discourse of the body, in which one discerns the beginnings of a primitive materialism. The aesthetic is the locus of all human subjectivity in early capitalist society, and survives in its pristine, animist form in the neo-idealism so familiar to us from the work of Borges. In pre-industrial

---

[13] See Viñas [1964], 253.
[14] See Rodríguez, 81-82.

economies, such as those of Spain and its colonies, culture was arrested at its artisanal stage, in which the subject remains "free" in its very being, rather than subservient to some oppressive external power. In short, it models its activity on the work of art. Such activity, however, presupposes a qualified return to the body; not its suppression but rather its spiritualization, since the body remains the transparent expression of the interior soul.

Although Platonism celebrates the joy of phenomena, it also circles around an absence, a black hole at the heart of language. Hence the anguish of imperfection which will lead the lyric poet – Borges is an especially striking example of this phenomenon – [15] in a vain attempt to express the ineffable, to grasp Truth in its quintessential form. Presence can be recovered only in memory, not through the nudes that Platonist ideology produces, since nudity here functions as a sign of a non-body, from which all matter has been cleansed. Refusal of presence is necessary under pain of incest. Speech and desire can never cohabit amicably, since meaning and being are mutually exclusive. To be more precise, the word can never express the object because the latter is rejected into an outside, beyond the reach of language. It is precisely this process that Garcilaso (and Borges) dramatizes in his verse. The binding of the sonnet – metrically one of the most exacting verse forms – is an imposition of the symbolic, which must resist the pressure of the fluid semiotic. The latter finds expression in Garcilaso in the maternal image of water – Borges will favour the mirror – in which we see ourselves reflected. However, as Narcissus discovered, an attempt at direct fusion leads to (the) death (language), which explains why the poet fears presence, when incarnated in (opaque) matter. Equally, the mother can only *be* by *abjecting* the child. [16]

The *alma bella* will not vary substantially in its transformation into the autonomous subject of a more developed capitalism for the simple reason that it is the function of the same mode of production. Within its pastoral enclave it carves out a space that the idealist will subsequently occupy, in flight from the alienation of modern society. In their equality of status both individual souls and subjects are complicit with the dominative instrumental thought of which they are the declared opponents; they are, in other words, examples

---

[15] See Gertel, 72-73.
[16] See Kristeva (1982).

of the very commodification that they attempt to resist. Similarly, the "plain," "universal" idiom that Borges will later recommend and cultivate has its origins in the humanistic discourse of the sixteenth century. Crucial to this discourse is the process by which words are stripped of their use value to become exchange value, that is, current "usage."[17]

As we have already emphasized, it is always necessary, when relating Borges to his predecessors in this way, to remain alert to the existence of innovation and discontinuity, and to avoid collapsing all differences into sameness. Thus, the modernist, a solitary monad within a grievously complex society, is not to be confused with the sixteenth-century courtier, who could still relate spontaneously and directly to the relatively simple social totality of which he was part. The former can recreate a lost wholeness only in the aesthetic, now marginalized by a division of labour which finds no place, in the productive process at least, for art; whereas the latter lay close to the sources of power, ever conscious of the need to ground politics in a refashioned culture and a revolutionized subjectivity.

Appreciation of such discontinuities sensitizes us to the existence of distinctive social structures and to the historical processes through which they are constantly transformed. An awareness of such transformation is particularly crucial to an understanding of sixteenth-century Spanish society, in which the bourgeoisie, while it inaugurates the division between the public and private sectors and thereby imposes severe restraints upon the activity of the nobility, surrenders control of the public sphere, increasingly after 1550, to feudal organicism. Politically, this compromise assumes the form of Absolutism, in which the humanistic pursuit of social harmony through the operations of the free spirit succumbs to the rationalist imposition of stability by a State legality. In linguistic terms, the preoccupation with law and concept as against sense and feeling is implied in the reduction of surface usage to deep structures.[18]

The retreat and eventual defeat of the bourgeoisie can be charted by a series of savage blows, which included the detention of Fray Luis de León in 1572, the placing of Huarte's work on the Index in 1583-4, and the virtual house arrest of Sánchez El Brocense at

---

[17] See Pozuelo Yvancos.
[18] See Padley (1976), 103-4 and passim.

about the same time.[19] Rationalism, which ideologically serves the coercive apparatus of State Absolutism, attempts to ground the social structure (including language) in metaphysical first principles. It affirms its hold less by a subtly consensual, ultimately more effective method of an aestheticizing neoplatonism than by abrasively direct, impositional means. The bourgeoisie, although firmly lodged in the Absolutist State, was unable in Spain to defend itself and to prevent the sacralization of the public sphere. With the practical disappearance of animism, a non-organicist Aristotelianism provided the only effective bulwark against organicism and the only viable basis from which to serve ideologically the mercantile relations which still existed at the economic level.

The contradictions to which these developments gave rise are most apparent in Fernando de Herrera, who in his *Anotaciones* on Garcilaso's poetry seeks to defend a Platonic practice by reference to Aristotelian theory.[20] Linguistically, the crisis point can be measured by a deepening uncertainty over the respective merits of the Platonic naturalist thesis (which, along with animism, is rooted in the medieval belief in spiritual manipulation) and the Aristotelian conventionalist thesis of scholastic derivation.[21] Both standpoints merge to constitute the Brocense's rationalist approach to language, which linguistic historians have failed to understand ideologically as an attempt at the legitimation of new trends through an appeal to non-organic Aristotelianism. Christian animists, let it be noted parenthetically, illustrate the same complexity. Fray Luis de León, for example, seeks to reconcile nominalist positions regarding language with neoplatonic poetics which, by emphasizing the divine harmony mirrored in poetry, is bound to presuppose the identity of words and things.[22]

V

The knowledge of this non-organicist Aristotelianism and of its obvious impact on the rationalism of Cervantes suggests that we treat with caution Borges' fascination with the playful juxtaposition

---

[19] See Blanco Aguinaga *et al.*, I, 281.
[20] See Rodríguez, 327 ff.
[21] See Read (1981), 90-92.
[22] See Read (1983), 131-4.

of literature and reality that characterizes the Spaniard's work. One understands the reason for the attraction. The projection of literature within literature corresponds in the modernist's own work with the idealist's sense of bodilessness, captured by the regressive vision of a thought within a thought, *ad infinitum:* "tales inversiones sugieren que si los caracteres de una ficción pueden ser lectores o espectadores, nosotros, sus lectores o espectadores, podemos ser ficticios" (OI, 68-69). Naturally enough, Borges assumes the motives of Cervantes and the modernist to be the same, namely to create a disquieting sense of mise-en-abyme: "Con cuentos que están dentro de cuentos se reproduce un efecto curioso, casi infinito, con una suerte de vértigo" (SN, 70). The same effect, he suggests, is created by the image of dreams that ramify and multiply endlessly.

But in a sense, of course, Borges is looking at Cervantes through the wrong end of the long telescope of time: during the Golden Age the bourgeoisie was struggling to consolidate its ascendency, whereas Borges views his predecessor after this class has run its historical course. Borges writes at a time when the free, autonomous subject of classical liberalism is under threat: Cervantes marks "a curious structural halfway house in the history of the subject, between its construction in bourgeois individualism and its disintegration in late capitalism" (Jameson [1979], 59). This would help explain a very close kinship between Borges' agonic couples and Don Quixote and Sancho: "They remain legal subjects who nonetheless lack genuine autonomy and find themselves obliged to lean on one another in a simulation of psychic unity which is little better than neurotic dependency" (59). It is in the nature of binary pairs, however, including that opposition formed by Borges and Cervantes themselves, to remain eternally locked in opposition, unless they are set in motion dialectically and, more importantly, returned to the historical context from which they emerged. Only then can we fully appreciate both the similarities and the differences which their status as mirror images implies.

In this respect, it is worth considering the work of Cervantes' contemporary, the grammarian Gonzalo Correas (d. 1630?). Correas, who extended the Brocense's rationalist method to the analysis of the vernacular, organized the rearguard defence of the crumbling intellectual edifice of humanism. By stabilizing and fixing syntactical structures, he bolstered the free subject and an exchange model of language entirely consonant with the bourgeois enterprise. He resists tenaciously the attempts by aristocratic poets to subvert this fixed rationalist order:

> Y quanto la orazion fuere guardando la dicha orden natural, ira mas clara, propia, dulze, i grave. I es mas lexitimo i propio estilo este de la lengua Kastellana, que de la Latina i Griega, i mas conforme al umor Español, y lengua Hebrea. No entendiendo esto algunos modernos escritores i poetas, a su parezer cortesanos cultos, enrredan de manera su lenguaxe i conzetos, que hablan en xerigonza, i huien de hablar Kastellano, claro i bueno: sino bastardeando con un poco de Latin, o Italiano que saben. La lengua para que es, sino para darse a entender i declararse sin pesadumbre. (Correas, 111)

At the same time, of course, Correas shows himself, through his authoritarianism and his rejection or marginalization of the aesthetic, to be complicit with an absolutist, centralized power intent on assuming the burdens of continuous supervision. The internalized self-discipline exercised by the bourgeois subject has been progressively displaced by external Authority, the effect of which is to jeopardize a market economics dependent for its smooth functioning on an autonomous subject.

Correas' ideal of transparent usage was given classical status through the work of Cervantes. The touchstone of this status, according to Borges, is a book's capacity to transcend, and so to escape, material contamination by the words on the page: ".[L]a página que tiene vocación de inmortalidad puede atravesar el fuego de las erratas [. . .] sin dejar el alma en la prueba" (D, 48). Hence, so the argument runs, the diaphanous quality of the Quixote's textual body.

However, whatever the similarities between Borges and Cervantes, which Borges himself is eager to emphasize, it is their differences, explicable ultimately in terms of their different social circumstances, that are most striking. If Cervantes systematically decodes the conventional behaviour and beliefs of a society geared to an archaic mode of production, it is in order to further the interests of the bourgeoisie.[23] His goal was not simply to unnerve the reader in

---

[23] See Jameson (1981), 152.

order to instil a sense of emptiness, of non-being, but to rise rationally above subjective knowledge towards an objective understanding of natural law, and, by extension, to press the claim of a reality that, however mystified by aristocratic design, was decidedly *there*. But he and his kind failed to thwart a Baroque obscurity which reasserts the diglossia essential to the preservation of the existing relations of production. The victory of the nobility blocks the full development of the productive forces of society and preludes the economic collapse of Spain.

VI

The rhetorical technique whereby a fiction is projected within a larger fiction and similar such devices employed by Borges have led critics to locate the Argentinian writer within the baroque movement that, historically, preceded the eventual triumph of bourgeois neo-classicism. Wheelock, for example, writes: "Borges is rightly called a Baroque writer. The Baroque is, essentially, a time or a circumstance in which the creative intellect ceases to find value in the results of thought and turns to contemplating the form of its own activity" (Wheelock, 8). Such views, we believe, call for serious qualification. For while it is true that Cervantes questions the relationship between fiction and reality, he does so not to subvert the plain style, but, on the contrary, to defend its merits at a time when it was still only one mode of writing among other modes, with which it was actively competing. The subjection of language to norms was one way of excluding these other, ultimately class-based modes. The bourgeoisie sought to present its own vision as the ultimate grounding, the Nature from which all else springs, to which end its novelists masked the ideological basis of their own practice at the same time that they demythologize that of their opponents. The defeat of the bourgeoisie, at the hands of aristocracy, was accompanied by the proliferation of genuinely baroque styles, also, to be sure, intent upon discovering "reality," but not that of some aspirant middle class. In these styles, animist logic has been reduced to a residual form, overlain by the substantialist thinking of organicism. Borges' relationship to them has been complex and shifting.

Of all baroque writers, the one with which Borges has most identified is undoubtedly Quevedo. Quevedo exhibited "una austera desconfianza sobre la eficacia del idioma" (I, 43), as part of a medieval assault upon (bourgeois) civilization. He does not operate upon a definable "outside," upon the world of referents: "La grandeza de Quevedo es verbal" (OI, 56). His descriptions of contemporary society, made from an organicist standpoint, are visions of hell, that explode internally. The ensuing destruction proves all the greater for its being contained. Torn asunder is the plain style of the bourgeoisie, a class destructive of the nobility's traditional privileges and whose racially impure origins Quevedo was out to expose. Sadistically, he disorders the symbolic, fritters away hoarded energy, and returns a pretentious intellect to its stinking body. In the process, the Oedipal complex is dismantled and the place of the transcendental subject inundated by a surge of *jouissance*.

A Cabbalistic strain surfaces in Quevedo's art of defamiliarization: "El quevedismo es psicológico: es el empeño en restituir a todas las ideas el arriscado y brusco carácter que las hizo asombrosas al presentarse por primera vez al espíritu" (I, 45). In a scintillating display of verbal acrobatics, words are restored, in the rubble of Babel, to something resembling their Edenic fullness. By a curious paradox, however, the explosive technique of *conceptismo* unleashes a materiality which mortgages Quevedo to bourgeois ideology just as effectively as it distances him from it. Words that have lost all intrinsic meaning, dissipated in a play of correspondences, demonstrate the same eccentric qualities of the commodity: their being is always elsewhere.

This over-determination leads to contradiction in other contexts, such as Quevedo's discussion of the history of Castilian. His utopianism is associated with the belief in his language's Babel origins – Quevedo's source is Gregorio López Madera (fl. 1601) – and its expansion, in historical times, from the mountainous provinces of the north. (Quevedo himself, not by chance, was of northern aristocratic extraction.) The Babelist devolutionary theory treats history in substantialist terms, as an entropic process, involving a descent into the inertia of matter. Such a degenerative view equates "substantial virtue" with stillness. Animism survives in Babelism in the form of a Platonic, Cratylean overlay. Castilian scholars are hard pressed to account for the confessedly crude linguistic forms of early documents. To assuage his anal anxieties, Quevedo, along with other Babelists, emphasizes the division between purity of thought and the bodily dross of language itself. Not surprisingly, he is attracted to Fray Luis de León, not simply for his clarity of style but for his ascetic rejection of the "world," by which we should understand the commercial vanities of bourgeois culture.[24]

Nothwithstanding his attraction to Madera's Babelist thesis, Quevedo's allegiance was ultimately to the court, whose imperialist designs found expression, linguistically, in Bernardo de Aldrete's "Latinist" thesis (1606) concerning the origins of Castilian. In this thesis, an animist emphasis on movement and change and a neoplatonic satisfaction with earthly things, including the vernacular, survives in a non-organicist Artistotelian guise. Unaccountably, Quevedo saw no contradiction between the Babelist view and Aldrete's imperialist model ("la lengua sigue al imperio").

Although Quevedo's conservatism is partly retrospective, it does not look finally to any polymorphously perverse body of Adam or of childhood. The organic community that Quevedo would recreate belongs to the Middle Ages. However reactionary and oppressive politically, such utopianism cannot be dismissed as simply an ideological perversion.[25] There is more at issue than the anxiety, even anguish, that characterizes any period of major historical change. The destruction of the medieval commune spelt disaster not merely for the traditional aristocracy but for the many whom it protected and whose basic needs it met, in however primitive a fashion. For such people, the "freedom" preached by the rising bourgeoisie translated into material impoverishment and social alienation. Nor must the attendant spiritual deformation be underestimated. For despite its asceticism, medieval culture preserved an earlier, less dehumanized stage in phylogenetic development which Quevedo rediscovered, in a somewhat debased and diluted form, to be sure, in his satanic, carnivalesque visions.

Naturally enough, Góngora was another baroque poet to attract Borges' attention. Like Quevedo, his poetry shows the subversive effects of the semiotic vis-à-vis the paternal function of syntax.[26] However, in contrast to Quevedo, a residual animism is much more in evidence in Góngora, with the result that the semiotic network is more or less integrated into the signifier. The dominance of sound symbolism over the aggression of the anal drives accounts for a

---

[24] For a more detailed discussion, see Read (1990), chapter 2.
[25] See Blanco Aguinaga et al., I, 388-9.
[26] For a more detailed discussion, see Read (1990), chapter 3.

characteristic oralization that mediates "between the fundamental sadism of rejection and its signifying sublimation" (Kristeva [1984], 153). Whereas Quevedo's verse ultimately bolsters the paternal law, Góngora's traces the patterns of the feminine *chora,* through the very distortion of words and syntagms. Not surprisingly, this union with the maternal body is achieved only at a considerable cost to linguistic "exchange," to the reified tokens of conventional discourse, and indeed to the very logicality of rationalist grammar.

As with Quevedo, however, Góngora rebels against the mimetic impoverishments of language only to fall victim to the very instrumentalizing tendencies that he sets out to thwart. In his case the ramifications of the paradox are particularly striking. Projected onto the social body, an emphasis upon the critical labour that poetic obscurity demands finds the poet in alliance with the rural sector, consisting of a marginalized, anti-mercantilist aristocracy and an exploited peasantry, against the urban world of commerce.[27] Rusticity preserves those sensual qualities lost under market-economy conditions which reduced the body itself to a reified, saleable product. Linguistically, its pre-capitalist values find expression in the kind of Adamic language that Góngora seeks to recreate. Artisanal activity corresponds with the reader's need to "work" the poetry. By the same token, however, Góngora's craftmanship forces the reader beyond all natural limits, after the manner of those courtly imperialists condemned by the poet for their overweaning pride. The result of such extravagance is a total fetishization of language and the hypostasis of the work of art as a material object. Thus, in a final paradoxical twist, poetry evades consumerism only to fall more firmly into its grasp.

In sum, Góngora serves an aristocracy unable in the long run to relinquish its exploitative, consumer role vis-à-vis the direct producers. It is this class allegiance that accounts for the poet's progressive pursuit of the "perfection" of Spanish, a pursuit that can only correspond with the activity of the court. Linguistic aggrandizement correlates with the conquest not only of the New World but of the rural sector within the old, with which the more traditional nobility otherwise had so much in common. Such an ideologically contradictory standpoint on the part of Góngora leads to

---

[27] See Beverley, 35.

unfinished masterpieces and a Faustian protagonist, as in *Las soledades,* unable to find a niche in society.

Borges' attraction to Quevedo is symptomatic of his involvement in avant-garde movements in the 1920s. The kind of futuristic art that appealed to Borges and his friends was notable for its anti-bourgeois sentiments, and had obvious appeal to a group of young poets intent on subverting the language of the previous generation. Needless to say, these sentiments were characteristically idealistic, not least of all in the philosophical sense of this term. Borges praises, for example, the attempt by the *conceptista* to "seguir con más veracidad las corvaduras de un pensamiento complejo" (I, 107), and even at this stage tries to distance himself from linguistically more disruptive styles: "[H]ay una más entrañable y conmovedora valía en las rebuscas del pensar que en las vistosas irregularidades de idioma" (I, 107). The revolutionary zeal of Borges' youthful romanticism remains in his enthusiasm for a kind of muted *jouissance* which, in the finest examples of *conceptismo,* leaves untouched the stable structure of patriarchal, symbolic order: "Son claros [los versos de Unamuno], pero su claror no es comparable al de un árbol que albrician en primavera las hojas, sino a la trabajosa claridad de una demonstración matemática" (I, 107).

However, in social terms, Borges' and Quevedo's positions are far from coinciding. For whereas Quevedo, the aristocrat, equates dirt with the aspirant bourgeoisie, Borges seeks, through his idealism, to distance himself from a working-class intent on wresting hegemony from the decadent bourgeoisie to which he himself belonged. And as Borges' class anxieties increased, his enthusiasm for Quevedo waned: "creo que yo tenía una admiración excesiva por Quevedo" (Sorrentino, 97). Indeed, in his later life Borges openly regretted his fascination with "los juegos de palabras bobos" (97) of the baroque poet. Such verbal pyrotechnics were scarcely compatible with the universal pretensions of the bougeoisie, epitomized by its "plain style."[28]

While the similarities between *gongorismo* and modern formalism have often been noted, Góngora, unlike Quevedo, could never really have proved very amenable to so trenchant an idealist as Borges, upon whom the connections, however subterranean and in-

---

[28] See Irby *et al.,* 35.

direct, between the body politic and the textual body were never lost. The baroque poet takes pleasure in the somatic dimensions of the sign, in the sensuous residue that eludes the oppressive rule of reason. Borges was too precariously poised socially to delight in such subjective passions, which are always liable to take a radical turn. At the same time, a sonnet by Góngora, which depended for its effect on the contorted emplacement of words, was implicated in aristocratic hegemony to a degree that was anathema to a poet such as Borges who had so actively resisted an aristocratic *modernismo* in his formative years. The sterile "palabra hojarasca" of such *culteranos* as Rimbaud, Swinburne, and Herrera y Reissig had, in his view, little to recommend it (I, 107); and if, in later years, he preferred Góngora to Quevedo, he still dismissed the Andalusian's mature works as a "perversión literaria" (Sorrentino, 98).

With his ideological shift to the right, Borges abandoned the baroque attempt to find a true, Adamic language. Increasingly his allegiance lay with the (spiritual) voice, not with the (bodily) script. Like any good idealist, he finally conceded that the thing-in-itself was beyond reach, at least the reach of words. "Una rosa amarilla" explores the dilemma whereby the birth of the symbol occasions the death of the body, and, conversely, whereby the authentic (re)discovery of reality proves language to be inherently inauthentic. It describes, to be more precise, how genuine poetic insight, in the baroque poet Giambattista Marino, induces silence, and how, coincidentally and in accordance with the same paradoxical logic, the poet's death heralds his accession to archetypal status in life eternal:

> Entonces ocurrió la revelación. Marino *vio* la rosa, como Adán pudo verla en el Paraíso, y sintió que ella estaba en su eternidad y no en sus palabras, y que podemos mencionar o aludir pero no expresar y que los altos y soberbios volúmenes que formaban en un ángulo de la sala una penumbra de oro no eran (como su vanidad soñó) un espejo del mundo, sino una cosa más agregada al mundo. (H, 44)

Platonism of this kind stands at odds with the spirit of the Baroque, which emphasizes the material density of language. Once it is accepted that reality cannot be reached through language, the sense of urgency is lost: syntactic convolutions give way to the transparent style of neo-classicism. At the same time, the baroque vision is not entirely dispensed with. It is preserved in Borges' fictional phantasmagoria, in which different planes of reality constantly shift and overlap, and a dense network of symbols and spiralling movements of infinite regression alienate the individual from any sense of rootedness: "Desgraciadamente, mis cuentos son barrocos en ese sentido" (Irby *et al.,* 35). The kaleidoscopic luxuriance of the baroque, as we shall see, feeds into a Romanticism which, while also seemingly relinquished by Borges in favour of neo-classicism, survives at the heart of his fictional creations. Here lies the fundamental truth of the claim that Borges is a baroque writer.

CHAPTER III

MONSTERS OF ENLIGHTENED REASON

I

Although French thought flourished in the seventeenth and eighteenth centuries, it did so within the parameters set by the centralized, Absolutist State, and, not surprisingly, reproduced within itself some of the tensions that were discernible in French society at large. Cartesian philosophy intitiates a move away from a perspectival, concrete reality to a view of the world *sub specie aeternitatis*, as a result of which a rift opens up between word and thing. While elevation of this kind prevents the soul, now transformed into a full subject, from being overwhelmed by the world, it burdens him/her with an increasingly abstract, and therefore devitalized, language. The body is put to sleep; to be is merely to think. And so, a subject distinguished by its capacity for existence finds itself deprived of all sense of substantial being.

The subjective consequences of Cartesian philosophy, in all their gravity, are only really apparent in the *Pensées* of Pascal, a work close to Borges' heart. In an essay entitled "La esfera de Pascal," the Argentinian writer presages his subsequent fictions by applying a model of agonic conflict to the encounter between the Ptolemaic and Copernican systems. The Copernican system, a superior archetypal fiction, surpasses the inferior narrative structure of the Greek astronomer. This dénouement recapitulates the success of the bourgeoisie in France, unlike in Spain, in blocking attempts by the nobility to undermine its relations of production. The ideological structure of Petrarchan animism, which sustained these relations in the first, mercantilist phase of capitalism, finds legitimation in and mutually influences the scientific work within the Copernican tradition. As a result, the new science is strongly coloured by the neoplatonic religion of numbers and the cult of sun worship. In contrast to the Ptolemaic system, which was closely bound to medieval organicism, the heliocentric model allowed for the interaction between the soul of the world and the soul of the spheres, and thereby for the radically transformative processes that were indispensable to the functioning of animism.[1]

As Borges indicates, in its early stages the shift from the spherical, boxed-in universe to the more open paradigm was experienced as a liberation, whereas subsequently, for Pascal, the sense of limitlessness in Copernicus induced a kind of cosmic dizziness coupled with feelings of fear and loneliness (OI, 13-17). Undoubtedly, such feelings indicate a transferral to the Creator of the inscrutability which the Renaissance neoplatonic poet experienced before his Lady (who assumed in late animism all the trappings of the Absolute). The nub of the fear for the Jansenist, as for the Protestant in general, is the question as to whether he is one of the elect or one of the eternally damned.

The buoyant optimism of an ascendant, expanding bourgeoisie – the engine room of what Borges describes as an "edad viril" (OI, 16) – found expression in the cosmic freedom experienced by such new converts to Copernicus' theory as Giordano Bruno (Borges' example). Linguistically, the optimism was embodied in a language professedly less rooted in a static nature, and which moved inexorably towards its perfection. This dynamism has gone in Pascal, whose cosmic experience of being adrift was related, in linguistic terms, to a radical dissociation between the component elements of language. Pascal believed that signifiers had been separated from the mental concepts (signifieds) that they pretend to represent and that signs no longer denote referents by virtue of any natural relationship "but only begin to represent them with the intervention of the subject" (Howe, 122).[2] To what do we attribute Pascal's pessimism and his sense of alienation?

The deep spiritual anguish that permeates Pascal's thought, his conviction of man's powerlessness before an all-powerful God, is rooted in the social experience of the *noblesse de robe,* a group to which he belonged through religious allegiance, as a convert to

---

[1] See Rodríguez, 70-73; and Tealdi, 45-63.
[2] See also Norman, 115-16.

Jansenism, and through class affiliation, as a member of the bourgeoisie.³ The frustration of these court nobles was that of a middle class unable to wrest political power from the monarchy and institute conditions favourable to its own development. Their loyalty to a monarch whose absolutism was making them politically irrelevant corresponds, theologically, with their blind faith in a God who is both hidden and omnipotent, whereas their emphasis on the autonomy of the individual is part and parcel of a newly discovered confidence in the power of reason.

The Jansenists' social marginalization is reflected in the linguistic philosophy of Port-Royal, a Jansenist institution. While much indebted to medieval scholasticism, and in particular to Augustinianism, Port-Royal grammar breaks with that of its predecessors in one important respect: unlike the scholastic, who had insisted on the link between language and the real world ("grammatica est signis rerum"), the seventeenth-century grammarian ignores the role of the referent. In other words, the traditional tripartite view of the sign (things, concepts, and words) is surrendered in the classical period for a binary view of the sign (concepts and words) which effectively brackets out its social context.⁴

II

In England the Puritans carried through the kind of revolution for which the French middle class had to wait till 1789. The Civil War (1640-60) enabled the bourgeoisie to acquire precisely sufficient political power so as to institute a regime propitious to its own economic well-being and advancement. Intellectually, its success gave rise to scientific empiricism which, in contrast to continental rationalism, insists on the isomorphism of language and reality. Empiricism represents a much more radical departure from organicist, substantialist notions than animism which constitutes for empiricists a compromise with feudalism or indeed a variation of the same. It was disseminated through the Royal Society, whose emphasis on things and the senses featured distinctively in the British

---

³ See Goldmann, 26-27, 35-37, 220-3.
⁴ See Padley (1985), 234. I am particularly indebted to Padley's work in this chapter.

strand of universal grammar and language planners. Consider, for example, G. Dalgarno's *Ars signorum* (1661) and J. Wilkins' *Essay Towards a Real Character and Philosophical Language* (1668). Wilkins' project was at least to some extent a cooperative and purely British effort, on the part of a group of scholars at Oxford which included Dalgarno, Seth Ward and John Wallis.

The legacy of Renaissance humanism – suspicion of scholastic metaphysical verbiage – manifests itself in the seventeenth century in the neglect of syntax, and in a corresponding tendency to limit attention to the lexicographical level of language. Necessarily, the verb is downgraded in favour of the noun, as the principal word class. In Dalgarno, for example the former has only a minor status, whereas in Wilkins (as incidentally in Port-Royal scholarship), it is resolved into the copula and adjective. Both Wilkins and Dalgarno exhibit, in a typically English manner, a firm belief in the capacity of language to mirror things.

Borges approached the whole question of the universal language schemes from the standpoint of the Nature/Convention debate. Overtly, he considers the debate to be somewhat sterile, in view of the obvious rightness of the conventional thesis: "todos los idiomas del mundo [. . .] son igualmente inexpresivos" (OI, 140). After all, he argues, can one truly decide whether "moon" or "luna" is more meaningful? However, if the choice of a lexeme so singularly resonant with poetic overtones does not alert us to the possibility of a *volte-face* on Borges' part, past experience should warn us that this advocacy of the commonsensical view often preludes a covert shift towards its opposite. And this is precisely what happens in the present case. Wilkins' lexemes, he confesses, "no son torpes símbolos arbitrarios" (OI, 141). Indeed, it seems, Wilkins' system of forty categories, with their numerous sub-categories, possesses qualities reminiscent of the cabbala, a fact guaranteed to recommend it positively to Borges' attention.

Ideologically, the universal language schemes correspond in part with a desire to stabilize and legitimize bourgeois ascendency. The conquest of reality proceeds through the classification of objects, on the basis of their distinctive attributes. The emphasis upon qualitative, as distinct from quantitative, change, betrays a covert desire less to change the world than to preserve it, to which end the category of nature is substituted for a convention more amenable to an aspirant class. At the same time, however, it is important to emphasize that this nature presupposes not a reinstatement of a material reality that convention had so effectively effaced, but rather a Platonic affirmation of language's underlying idealism. To this extent, Borges was both philosophically and historically justified in mentioning cabbalism in the context of the universal language schemes. For Wilkins' work represents a continuation of currents of medieval and Renaissance thought involving strongly mystical strains. Even within English empiricism of a hard-nosed variety, the seventeenth-century approach to Nature was still inextricably entangled with all kinds of occultism, astrology, alchemy, and magic, inherited from an earlier animism, that converge on a preoccupation with the virtues of an Adamic tongue.

By playing off nature and convention one against the other, Borges was able to highlight certain fundamental ambiguities present in classical thought, in which a would-be realistic approach based on the prior observation of facts is accompanied by a widespread nominalism subversive of any attempt to construct a one-to-one correspondence between name and referent. Empiricism rejects universals as mere "names" while simultaneously providing names for the "particulars" of the universe. The conviction is that symbols represent not words but refer directly to things, or at any rate to men's concepts of them. But Bacon's nominalism called into question the very *raison d'être* of seventeenth-century empiricism by questioning the link between concepts and things. For concepts must perforce be defined, and definitions, however detailed and complex, cannot renege on their status as language. On this basis, Wilkins' and other scholars schemes suffer from a basic circularity. Claiming to catalogue the real world as a preliminary to its symbolization, they take as their starting point the Aristotelian categories inherited from tradition, and then seek properties in phenomena to correspond to them. The problem is that reality cannot easily escape mediation, since it is not simply there, waiting to be seen, but must pass through the lens of language.

These tensions within classicism are explored with humour and to effect by Borges in his "Del rigor en la ciencia," in which he tells of an Empire whose cartographers were so sophisticated that their map of a province was equal to the size of a city, and their map of the Empire, to the size of a Province. The writer continues: "Con el tiempo, estos Mapas Desmesurados no satisficieron y los Colegios de Cartógrafos levantaron un Mapa del Imperio que tenía el

Tamaño del Imperio y coincidía puntualmente con él" (HI, 131-2). Needless to say, later generations abandoned it, finding it too cumbersome.

The point is, of course, that cartography – a science which made rapid advances in the classical period – is inescapably Platonic. Maps, like language, are effective only by virtue of their abstraction, that is, of their distance from reality. There is no gainsaying this fact, however repugnant to the Aristotelian. And repugnant it is: David the poet, we recall, was driven to suicide by being made to draw maps endlessly.

III

"I would attempt a kind of pure colorless eighteenth-century English," Borges advises Norman Thomas di Giovanni, one of his translators into English, even to the extent of excluding slang that "smacks of a particular place" (Giovanni *et al.,* 112). Such, of course, is the classic bourgeois rhetoric of innocence, which proclaims the freedom of the public sphere at the same time as it excludes from it the vast majority of citizens. In Borges' own day, when this sphere is under threat, and has indeed been invaded by the marginalized social body, there are virtues to a Convention that effectively minimizes the impact of a problematic material reality. Its appeal generates doubts in Borges concerning the validity of Alfred Korzybski's "penultimate version of reality," in which vegetable corresponds with length, animal with width, and human with depth. Such modern attempts at classification, he argues, presuppose like their neo-classical forerunners "una sabiduría que se funda, no sobre un pensamiento, sino sobre una mera comodidad clasificatoria, como lo son las tres dimensiones convencionales. Escribo *convencionales,* porque – separadamente – ninguna de las dimensiones existe: siempre se dan volúmenes" (D, 39-40).

Convention in the modern context serves the purpose not of an expansive bourgeoisie, intent upon breaking down the barriers of a closed feudal society, but of a class in retreat. It emphasizes the idealist dimension of classical thought, at the expense of its empiricist ambitions. Speculation has become a game, a mere pastime, unconcerned with the life we mistakenly call the real: "La imposibilidad de penetrar el esquema divino del universo no puede, sin embargo, disuadirnos de planear esquemas humanos, aunque nos conste que éstos son provisorios. El idioma analítico de Wilkins no es el menos admirable de esos esquemas" (OI, 143). In this way, Borges, whose own concerns are strictly with the spirit, interprets classical thought as shunning the referent in order to turn in upon itself. It is no longer the empiricist aspects of the universal language schemes that fascinate him but their quality of the fantastic or marvellous, and the improbable: "Teóricamente, no es inconcebible un idioma donde el nombre de cada ser indicara todos los pormenores de su destino, pasado y venidero" (OI, 143).

It is only a short step from claiming that language has no direct access to the thing-in-itself to claiming that this thing does not exist and that language does not bear the onus of referring to a reality outside of itself. The classicist is thereby saved any concern with the real world, a view which became increasingly attractive during the decline of the bourgeoisie. As Borges notes, "los escritores de hábito clásico más bien rehuyen lo expresivo" (D, 67). Since Borges demands so little of language in the way of referential capability, he saves himself the despair of those who would have words refer to things. The referent has largely been omitted, and no longer taunts the speaker with its absence: "El clásico no desconfía del lenguaje, cree en la suficiente virtud de cada uno de sus signos" (D, 67). While Borges has in mind a transhistorical category of classicism, significantly he singles out Gibbon's *Decline and Fall,* from neo-classicism proper, with which to illustrate

> el carácter mediato de esta escritura generalizadora y abstracta hasta lo invisible. El autor nos propone un juego de símbolos, organizados rigurosamente sin duda, pero cuya animación eventual queda a cargo nuestro. No es realmente expresivo: se limita a registrar una realidad, no a representarla. Los ricos hechos a cuya póstuma alusión nos convida, importaron cargadas experiencias, percepciones, reacciones; éstas pueden inferirse de su relato, pero no están en él. Dicho con mejor precisión: no escribe los primeros contactos de la realidad, sino su elaboración final en conceptos. (D, 68)

Insofar as the solipsistic circle is never finally closed, Croce's expressive view survives residually in Borges' use of favourite concepts of neo-idealism, such as the necessity of imprecision and of an automatic selectivity in any linguistic process: "La simplificación conceptual de estados complejos es muchas veces una operación instantánea. El hecho mismo de percibir, de atender, es de orden selectivo: toda atención, toda fijación de nuestra conciencia, comporta una deliberada omisión de lo interesante" (D, 69). The noninteresting encompasses such complex, physical activities as breathing and crossing the street: "Nuestro vivir es una serie de adaptaciones, vale decir, una educación del olvido" (D, 70). But more crucially, it penetrates to the core of language itself. The Convention that rules language is an institutionalized forgetting. Gibbon's metaphors are not without good reason *public* metaphors. Consider, for example, his phrase "reign of silence":

> Naturalmente, la justifica su invisibilidad, su índole ya convencional. Su empleo nos permite definir otra de las marcas del clasicismo: la creencia de que una vez fraguada una imagen, ésta constituye un bien público. Para el concepto clásico, la pluralidad de los hombres y de los tiempos es accesoria, la literatura es siempre una sola. (D, 70)

The pattern of Borges' subsequent career is thus set: increasingly he dispenses with a key Romantic element of idealism, namely its sense of lack and its frustration at the inability of language to capture the real. Taking a Romantic neo-idealism, in which a privatized individual struggles with the sheer publicity of language, in an effort to express his feelings exactly, he transforms it into a kind of classicism which dispenses with the whole notion of referents. By doing so, he avoids the possibility of dissatisfaction with the insufficiency of language. At the same time, however, by calling into question the empiricist assumption that language opens out directly upon the world, Borges' brand of idealism de-stabilizes the whole classical episteme. This episteme presupposed a structural fixity intrinsic to which was the pre-eminence of the noun. An idealistic romanticism which privileges the fluidity of the verb exposes the provisionary, partial basis of the classical tables and systems of nomenclature, which otherwise assume the mantle of eternity. There simply exists no neutral ground upon which such classifications can be erected, except in the form of a Chinese encyclopedia that divides animals into (a) belonging to the Emperor, (b) stuffed, (c) tame, (d) fabulous, (e) that behave as if they are mad, (f) that are innumerable, (g) that are drawn with the brush of a fine camel hair, etc. The force of such an argument is irresistible: "no hay clasificación del universo que no sea arbitraria y conjetural. La razón es simple: no sabemos qué cosa es el universo" (OI, 142-3).

In sum, Borges' classicism is the product of a purely contemplative view of the world. It postulates a knowledge to which one accedes directly, without any practice/praxis, a pre-existent Truth that simply awaits categorization and cataloguing. In the absence of any movement or mediation between subject and object, this truth can be acquired only through a cold gaze that scans motionless, remote objects silently arranged in space and which, it transpires, are nothing less than the mute projection of the subject's own internal abstractions.

IV

The literary genre which most closely corresponds to medieval Realism, as Borges himself discerns (OI, 215), is allegory, which substitutes the realm of the Ideal for noumenal reality. Any nominalist – and, by Borges' own estimation, we moderns are nominalists by reflex – is bound to find allegory somewhat irresponsible. For far from struggling to interpret the world, the nominalist will argue, such protestant writers as Bunyan discover a meaning that is there from a start. Whereas a medieval allegorist such as Dante acknowledges the necessity of including the referent, his protestant counterpart feels able to dispense with it, in favour of a strictly binary view of language, and, in the process, to dispense with the objective world. There exists for him no sense of tension, of an obligation to match the subjective world with its material counterpart. Allegory "does not account for the opposition it sets up between light and darkness, good and evil, and so on, it merely states it" (Josipovici, 146).

Borges' own reservations notwithstanding, he proceeds to commit one of those furtive *volte-faces* to which we have grown accustomed in similar contexts: "me gustaría saber cómo pudo gozar de tanto favor una forma que nos parece injustificable" (OI, 211). Allegory, in Borges' view, is not as dispensable as it might initially seem. Its relationship with the novel, for example, is far from clearcut. On the face of it, both genres are diametrically opposed: allegory, born of medieval realism, is a "fábula de abstracciones," whereas the novel, with its roots in nominalism deals with the specific individual. But, as Borges continues, it is by no means easy to separate opposites. Allegory and the novel, like nominalism, and realism, are mirror images of each other: "Las abstracciones están personificadas; por eso, en toda alegoría hay algo novelístico. Los individuos que los novelistas proponen aspiran a genéricos (Dupin es la Razón, Don Segundo Sombra es el Gaucho); en las novelas hay un elemento alegórico" (OI, 215).

What needs to be emphasized is the ideological complexity of such generic discussion. Allegory is an expression of medieval substantialism, in which symbols take the full force of literal meaning, in the tradition of the *Cratylus*. By the same token, it also continues that idealism which was characteristic of this Platonic standpoint in its earliest forms, through the creation of an allegorical realm consisting neither of "words" nor "things" but of personified "essences." Conversely, the novel is the bourgeois genre *par excellence*, which reveals the subject-centredness of the bourgeois matrix, particularly in its classical phase. The novel's purely conventional signs are universalized, that is, are "naturalized," through the need to legitimate the bourgeoisie's cultural hegemony. Given the neo-idealist dispersal of the subject, Borges predictably inclines in his own art to the short-story form, as opposed to the novel, since it permits a more (philosophically) realistic practice. The weak ego that this realism presupposes precludes individual "psychologizing," analysis of character types, and personal introspection, on the basis of which medieval and post-modern practices emerge as specular opposites, caught in an endless play of difference and identity.

Notably enlightening in this context is Borges' short story "El acercamiento a Almotásin," which, in a sense, prepares the ground for the subsequent stories that were to make him famous. This story takes a meta-critical form, as a review of a novel. In his typically ironic manner, Borges has the reviewer adopt the standpoint of mimetic realism, that is to say, a standpoint directly opposed to his own. Accordingly, the 1932 version of the book under review is criticized for its mimetic insufficiency – Almotásin, for example, "tiene su algo de símbolos" (F, 42). In the 1934 version, to the reviewer's regret, the book has assumed the form of a full-blown allegory.

Allegory, then, and the realistic mode that sustains it, triumphs through its idealistic form. It establishes a realm cleansed of contingency, elevates above disorder and chaos a nature that is the acme of sublimation. Yet organicism is bound to the body, which it views relentlessly through the prism of anality, and which, in its corruptibility, dogs the allegorical protagonist: "Dice otras cosas viles y menciona que hace catorce noches que no se purifica con bosta de búfalo" (39). Through him, the most dematerialized of genres is scarred by ambiguities of sexual identity and images of castration: "Sube por una escalera de fierro – faltan algunos tramos – y en la azotea, que tiene un pozo renegrido en el centro, da con un hombre escuálido, que está orinando vigorosamente en cuclillas, a la luz de la luna" (39). The consequences, in linguistic terms, are no less paradoxical. For while, within the sanctuary of the individual work, Borges aspires to an ontologically full and unarbitrary discourse, the ultimate origin of things, upon which this discourse closes, can only be the disembodied voice of Almotásin.

V

In a number of short stories, Borges explored one of the key problems of seventeenth- and eighteenth- century scholarship, namely the idealistic basis of scientific empiricism. "Funes el Memorioso," for example, focuses on the (in)capacity of language to refer to reality. Prior to his accident, Funes was distanced from life within a living body: "miraba sin ver, oía sin oír, se olvidaba de todo" (F, 127). After his accident, his newly discovered proximity to life ("el presente era casi intolerable de tan rico y tan nítido" [127]) coincides with a loss of material contact. A vision of eternity is permitted only to those who "abject" the body. To meet Funes, the narrator must journey down the winding labyrinth of the bowels. He exits into a higher realm of the spirit, which, needless to say, the idealist attempts to pass off as elemental matter: "Resonaron las sílabas romanas en el patio de tierra" (126).

Funes pursues his goal of total proximity through a language of his own device, with which to circumvent the habitual abstraction of ordinary language. This, as the narrator explains, rather defeats the founding principle of language, which is abstract in its essence:

> Locke, en el siglo XVII, postuló (y reprobó) un idioma imposible en el que cada cosa individual, cada piedra, cada pájaro y cada

rama tuviera un nombre propio; Funes proyectó alguna vez un idioma análogo, pero lo desechó por parecerle demasiado general, demasiado ambiguo. En efecto, Funes no sólo recordaba cada hoja de cada árbol, de cada monte, sino cada una de las veces que la había percibido o imaginado. Resolvió reducir cada una de sus jornadas pretéritas, a unos setenta mil recuerdos, que definiría luego por cifras. Lo disuadieron dos consideraciones: la conciencia de que la tarea era interminable, la conciencia de que era inútil. (129-30)

Funes, however, remains unrepentant. In his unflinching allegiance to the concrete, he combines an extreme Aristotelianism with a neo-idealism of Romantic vintage. As a result, he makes imposible demands upon a medium by defininition incapable of ontological fullness, whose only virtues are those of generality:

[. . .] era casi incapaz de ideas generales, platónicas. No sólo le costaba comprender que el símbolo genérico *perro* abarcara tantos individuos dispares de diversos tamaños y de diversa forma; le molestaba que el perro de las tres y catorce (visto de perfil) tuviera el mismo mombre que el perro de las tres y cuarto (visto de frente). (130).

In the particular case of Funes, the power of intelligence does not coincide with comprehension. Knowledge is achieved not through the dialectical interplay of subject and object, not through a process of mediation which necessarily involves language. It arrives, like some supernatural visitation, in a sudden intuition, the price of whose immediacy is a break, through illness, with the life of praxis.[5]

Through Funes the idealist's dream came true, but it turned out to be not heaven but hell on earth. Clearly, we can be reunited with mother/matter only in death. The detour through life depends upon our capacity to forget, or, which is the same thing, to sleep: "Dormir es distraerse del mundo" (131). Necessarily, language escapes the insomniac: "Había aprendido sin esfuerzo el inglés, el francés, el portugués, el latín. Sospecho, sin embargo, que no era muy capaz de pensar. Pensar es olvidar diferencias, es generalizar, abstraer. En el abarrotado mundo de Funes no había detalles, casi inmediatos" (131). Unless we withdraw from libidinal contact with

---

[5] See Tealdi, 68-69.

the world, reality overwhelms us, as it finally overwhelmed Funes: he dies of mental, or rather physical, congestion.

Whatever Borges' inadequacies in strictly philosophical terms, and there are some critics who believe that they are radical,[6] his charge of idealism against Locke is substantially correct, and by no means irrelevant to an understanding of seventeenth-century ideas on language. Although like any self-respecting empiricist-cum-sensualist, Locke believed that Ideas derived from things, he understood nouns as standing primarily for Ideas in the mind, as opposed to things in the real world. In consequence, there is little in practice, of for that matter in theory, to separate his "internal operations of our minds" from the rationalist's "operations of the spirit." The empiricist's emphasis on sense impressions is neutralized by the fact that, despite appearances, he is concerned primarily not with real but with nominal essences of things. Finally, therefore, he suffers from a loss of contact with reality, and from the solipsism that awaits anyone who would ignore things at the expense of words and concepts.

Locke's epistemological shortcomings help us understand more fully the outcome of "Funes el memorioso." Funes is reborn not into reality, whose eclipse is signalled by the total darkness which engulfs narrator and protagonist during their meeting, but into a dream world. Reality lies beyond the blocked windows, glimpsed, if at all, through an iron grid. Funes himself lies a prisoner, "inmóvil, con los ojos cerrados" (124); his body is dead, an inert adjunct of the mind, symptomatic of which is his "silent" face and elongated hands. Historically, such spiritual withdrawal corresponds with the transition from Locke to Berkeley and with the increasing idealism that characterizes the Anglo-Saxon tradition of philosophical empiricism, a fact not lost upon Borges: Funes' father, he is at pains to emphasize, was an Englishman with a touch of the Irish (O'Conner).

VI

"Tlön, Uqbar, Orbis Tertius" traverses much the same terrain as that covered in "Funes": scientific pretensions, based on an objective, one-to-one match between word and thing, are subverted by a

---

[6] For example, Blanco González, 41; Sábato, 69.

process of idealization. In addition, this story marks far more clearly the transition from noun to verb, as *the* principal part of speech, and consequently is far more compromised by Romantic idealism. In fact, it represents an expansion of Borges' "Chinese encyclopedia," which endeared him so much to post-structuralists such as Foucault.

"Orbis Tertius" is visibly rooted in the problematics of the Enlightenment. As a project, Tlön was initiated by a secret society associated with Dalgarno and Berkeley. Dalgarno, we have seen, was one of the early inventors of a universal language, whose aim was to recreate a new Adamic language. His appearance in Borges' fiction is due to more than chance: "[t]he same analytical language of Wilkins and the ordered world of Tlön are both expressions of the same yearning for an order that is unattainable to human intelligence" (Alazraki [1971 (ii)], 49). The encyclopedia, the means by which Tlön infiltrates our world, is the quintessential symbol, along with the dictionary, of the age of reason and the empiricist tradition. Bayle's *Dictionary* (1687) and Diderot's *Encyclopedia* (1751-) correspond with the incorporation of British thought by Continental scholarship, and indicate the strengthening of the bourgeoisie in France.

As in "Funes el memorioso," empiricism shows itself in "Orbis Tertius" to be deeply contaminated by idealism: revealingly, Tlön is modelled on the Cabbala (F, 31), whose Platonic sources we have already had cause to consider. For while Herbert Ashe is unable to forget – hence his fatal congestion (18) – his love of chess and mathematics is symptomatic of the abstraction that afflicts the whole encyclopedia project. This abstraction imposes a terrible alienation from reality, not least of all upon Ashe himself, whose very name expresses his dissociation from the life of the body.

The culture of Tlön confirms our claim that neo-idealism elevates words above the concrete circumstances in which they are actually used, in accordance with the Hegelian principle that being is thinking, and that empirical truth, under these conditions, is but an internal moment of the Idea. In their spiritualized form, words are but tokens of hypostatized abstractions. On the other hand, mental reality, in order to exist, must transform itself into real objects, and words reconnect with particular, corporeal forms. Once this is achieved, Borges is able to celebrate the transcendental coincidentally with the lived moment.[7] Needless to say, the Marxist is bound to interrogate the ideological sleight-of-hand involved whereby the empirical world is smuggled *uncritically* back into the Ideal, and, more specifically, an eternal category, "language," is substituted for an historically specific phenomenon, namely the class dialect.[8]

Tlön involves the most radical attempt to destroy the view of language as adequate to thing.[9] The encyclopedia is an arbitrary system, a fiction which, far from presenting a faithful mirror image of the real, deforms it, prior to dispensing with it in its entirety: "Su lenguaje y las derivaciones de su lenguaje – la religión, las letras, la metafísica – presuponen el idealismo" (F, 21). Its world is one of succession, not of spatiality, and consequently defies all attempts at categorization. It is, quite simply, inaccessible to substantives. For example, its southern dialects have no word for moon, only the verbs "lunecer" or "lunar." In contrast, the dialects of the north consist solely of adjectives, that is, constantly shifting attributes unattached to any essence. The ideal object becomes a chance conglomeration of such attributes which come together momentarily, as in the play of sunlight or the flow of water against the chest of the swimmer, only to be dissoved the next instance.

Tlön, we suggest, captures perfectly the transition from neoclassical structuralism to post-structuralism. It is the former that accounts for its initial appeal: "Casi inmediatamente, la realidad cedió en más de un punto" (35). Humanity was "[e]ncantada por su rigor." People are not only willing but longing to believe in a universe cleansed of material contingency. But this same humanity, the narrator reminds us, forgets that this rigour is the illusory creation of chess-players, not of angels. Its order is the mirror image of a dis-

---

[7] Compare Hegel's conclusion: "Thus consciousness on its onward path from the immediacy with which it began is led back to absolute knowledge as its innermost *truth*. This last, the ground, is then also that from which the first proceeds, that which at first appeared as an immediacy. This is true in still greater measure of absolute spirit which reveals itself as the concrete and final supreme truth of all-being, and which at the *end* of the development is known as freely externalizing itself, abandoning itself to the shape of an *immediate being* – opening or unfolding itself into the creation of a world which contains all that fell into the development which preceded that result and which through this reversal of its position relatively to its beginning is transformed into something dependent on the result as principle" (Hegel, 106).

[8] Cf. Marx (1975), 91, 98.

[9] See Bickel.

order that resists classification: "Todo estado mental es irreducible: el mero hecho de nombrarlo – *id est,* de clasificarlo – importa un falseo" (23). Slippage occurs between signifier and signified. The ice-fields of structuralism fracture and begin to flow. But, needless to say, Tlön's language is completely abstracted from any material context: if neo-idealism destabilizes all positivist science, and particularly mathematics, it does so not by reintroducing material flux, but through the *idea* of this flux.

VII

While the subversion of the fixity of symbolic positions, emphasized by idealism, threatens the integrity of the ego, it does so at a post-individual level, by which stage the loss of the body has deprived this ego of its material base. In consumer society, the progressive improvement of the individual, which sees his very being transferred to external objects or commodities, along with his social bond, is matched by an increasingly disembodied reality, whose sensuous, concrete activities and values are veiled by abstract categories of labour and exchange value.

The consequences of such abstraction, however mediated, are only too apparent within the realm of philosophical idealism: "Berkeley afirma: Sólo existen las cosas en cuanto se fija en ellas la mente. Lícito es responderle: Sí, pero sólo existe la mente como perceptiva y meditadora de las cosas. De esta manera queda desbaratada no sólo la unidad del mundo externo sino la espiritualidad" (I, 115). Berkeley's subject, intimately tied to God but lacking any relationship with an outside, is still very much the substantial "soul" inherited from animism. The transition from Berkeley to Hume that Borges describes corresponds with the destruction of this residual animism by empiricist ideology. In Hume, the process of fragmentation is carried through to the point at which the subject is itself negated, not in itself but as a "soul": "Ambos enormes sustantivos, espíritu y materia, se desvanecen a un tiempo y la vida se vuelve un enmarañado tropel de situaciones de ánimo, un ensueño sin soñador" (I, 115). By this stage, it seems, the subject possesses no substantial being as such, beyond its coincidence with a group of sensations.[10]

---

[10] See Rodríguez, 375.

Needless to say, the defeat of animism in Spain precluded any sustained development of empiricism. The Bourbons attempted to impose progressive measures, in tune with their own "enlightened" policies, but the continuing dominance of feudal interests within the public sphere prevents their radication. Similarly, independent moves by members of the bourgeoisie to affirm their own ideology had only a superficial effect: there was, for example, only one attempt in Spain (by Fr. Martín Sarmiento [1766]) to construct a scheme for a universal language. However, changes in material production *were* taking place which, together with important superstructural developments, were to lend to the animist tradition a curious modernity. I have in mind particularly the increasing commodification of artefacts in the market place and the consequent emergence of the aesthetic – a crucial text is Esteban de Arteaga's *La belleza ideal* (1789) – as an independent, autonomous category. It is important, both in itself and for my subsequent treatment of Borges, that these transformations are precisely understood.

The aestheticization of culture in the eighteenth century is symptomatic of problems increasingly encountered by authoritarian regimes. In Spain, as such writers as Cadalso, Forner, and even Jovellanos illustrate, the bourgeoisie continued to defer to, and to compromise with, an aristocracy which preserved many of its feudal trappings. These included a dictatorialism which, when blended with the entrepreneurial spirit of a more aggressive, self-assertive bourgeoisie found in Europe, sought to universalize its life-ways. Aesthetics in Spain answers the need of an absolutist State to achieve hegemony more indirectly, through the individual network of finer feelings, in a manner once practised by the neoplatonic animism that organicism has so effectively eclipsed in the Renaissance. This did not involve, it is important to realize, an abandonment of reason, but rather a more effective marketing of it. In this way social unease could be contained and potential revolutionary situations defused. The tactic is effective, but not without its dangers, as the subsequent history of idealism will show.[11]

Idealism, I suggested above, resumes the neoplatonic project; rather than producing a new kind of subject, it rediscovers the *alma bella* familiar to us from the earlier mercantilist phase of capitalism. Only now, of course, the historical circumstances have changed;

---

[11] See Eagleton (1990), 13 ff.

bourgeois egoism is threatening to carry all before it, in its philistinely utilitarian, insensitively abrasive manner. Aesthetics signals a move towards the feminization of discourse, and, in the same gesture, the subversion of the subject's phallic authority. At its subliminal moments, it does indeed transcend this ultimately dispensable category of individual identity. Borges himself will describe such a moment when, while wandering through the outlying suburbs of Buenos Aires, he sensed his own non-being (HE, 39-40). Possibly taking a cue from Schopenhauer, however, one of his favourite philosophers, he discovers that the individual can survive, indeed, can thrive, in the contemplation of its own death. With the dissipation of the great metaphysical concepts of space and (historical) time, the subject is "limitado a este vertiginoso presente" (I, 116). The modernist presses the classical idealist up to and beyond the ultimate embodiment of presence, presiding over the total implosion of identity: "Fuera vanidad suponer que ese agregado psíquico ha menester asirse a un yo para gozar de validez absoluta" (I, 85). Within this domain of narcissism, there exists no inside or outside, no subject or object, but only the sublimated flow of the drives.

Borges is drawn to idealist philosophy because of its anti-humanistic bias towards the subject: like his post-structuralist admirers, he gives up on the fully integrated individual (and on the author) as part of a last ditch attempt to salvage a superannuated liberalism.[12] Idealism is, in other words, the bridge over which he passed from modernism's predilection for myth and symbol and its presupposition of a relatively independent subject to a post-modernism responsive to the fictional sense of personal identity.[13] The post-modernist marks the limit of a process which we have already observed in the neoplatonic poet, whereby commodification reduces subjects themselves to abstract, disembodied, fictive entities, which can be interchanged at will. In this way idealistic transcendence and the bliss of nirvana, like so many noble things, show themselves to be rooted in the sordid practices of the market place.

---

[12] Cf. Eagleton (1984), 98-100.
[13] For more detail on the distinction between modernism and post-modernism see Williams (1989), 23, 130; and Russell, 242 ff.

VIII

One eighteenth-century writer whom Borges, in early essays remarkable for both their blindness and insight, tried unsuccessfully to enlist for his idealist cause was the satirist Diego de Torres Villarroel (1694-1770). As the post-modernist in Borges perceived, Villarroel's turbulent autobiography was the product of a subject which barely persisted as an integral unity through time and space, to the extent, indeed, that its author was a non-presence ("no era nadie" [I, 89]). However, unlike the idealist, Torres regresses to a pre-subjective stage in which the subject becomes enamoured of itself as *body,* not as mind. Borges himself seems to sense his own radical misprision: Torres' obscenities and crudities, the assault upon language, constitute an attempt to "enloquece[r] el pensamiento" (I, 11), in an act of intellectual vandalism totally at odds with neo-classical decorum and rationality. The prolonged screaming and joking ("esa violencia casi física de su verbo" [I, 11]) subvert that very realm of privacy that the idealist reserved for himself.

Indeed, in his extremity, Torres arrives at a position diametrically opposed to his idealist counterpart. Borges himself seems to concede as much when he concludes that the satirist lacked "esa ansia de eternidad" so typical of his antagonist (I, 13-14). The conclusion, however, is premature, and disappointing in one otherwise so attuned to the dynamics of agonic conflict. For even the most superficial reading of the *Vida* reveals an author concerned with fame and the issue of his own survival beyond death to the point of obsession. Death haunts Torres' very act of writing, not merely in the straightforward sense that, as he himself affirms, his work would provide material for his funeral rites, but, more subtly insofar as each addition to/ edition of his "life" is experienced as a triumph over death. Overwhelmed by material inertia, the satirist projects an inverted image of the spectral, insubstantial self of the idealist.[14]

Both bourgeois and Marxist critics have emphasized Villarroel's bourgeois provenance. Of course, there is much in Torres to support such an interpretation. For example, he lived off the proceeds from the sale of his books, had a firm notion of his property rights

---

[14] For a more detailed discussion of Villarroel, see Read (1990), chapter 5.

as author, and was suitably outraged by pirate editions of his work. Moreover, a willingness to allow his wit to be socially absorbed betrays itself in a petty-bourgeois upward fawning and class insecurity.

Such a critical perspective, however, does scant justice to the complexity of Torres, whose work demonstrates clearly the co-existence of different moments of socio-economic development. At a time when the bourgeoisie in its classic, empiricist phase was aggressively rationalizing the universe, in an attempt to gain control over its environment, Torres spoke to an earlier animism in which the individual passively registered external "influences." These influences, the intricacies of which are explored in his prognostics, almanacs, and calendars, lock Torres firmly into a feudal animism, concerned with the magical manipulation of spirits. The masks and disguises that he dons on different occasions celebrate the triumph of bodies and social signs which, while conceived as non-substantial, remain inscribed under sin and dirt.

While Torres registers the continuing influence within Spain of carnivalesque truancy, it is not the weak, collective ego of medieval culture that he was out to subvert but the autonomous "free" subject of the bourgeoisie, which Enlightenment rationalism was seeking to impose in Spain. Thus the satirist offers himself in his work as the irrepressible agent of the forces of rejection which flood the symbolic and overwhelm established theses. Not only does he make it possible to psychoanalyse the author but he positively invites it: "[. . .] porque a hurtadillas de mi vigilancia se han salido, arrebujados entre las expresiones, las bachillerías y las incontinencias, muchos pensamientos y palabras que han descubierto las manías de mi propensión y los delirios de mi voluntad" (Torres, 147). Nor should we lightly refuse his own self-analytical gambits, in particular the importance that he attributes to his feminine passivity or, as he terms it, his "docility" and "malleability." For perhaps the most striking symptom of his neurosis is his paranoia, an illness which is classically entangled with homosexuality.[15] On every side, he discerned "enemies" quietly undermining his position, sedulously plotting his ruin. Needless to say, Torres' insights, however symptomatic of his instability, were in all probability not lacking in percipience, in which respect he again exhibits the classic attributes of the paranoic.

---

[15] See Freud, "Schreber," IX, 129-223 (particularly section III).

The dynamics of Torres' neurosis, which includes a considerable degree of exhibitionism, are plainly visible and relatively easy to chart. As Freud bluntly expresses it (with respect to the Wolf Man): "The unconscious repressed homosexuality withdrew into his bowel." [16] In his unremitting obscenity, involving the exposure of the anal zone, Torres plays the woman's part while repudiating his need for an incestuous relationship with his father. Similarly, the importance that he attaches to being beaten, as a corrective for bad behaviour: "It is not only the punishment for the forbidden genital relationship, but also the regressive substitute for that relationship," [17] which explains why Torres was destined to act out his embivalence with a variety of surrogate Oedipal figures – his schoolmaster, the hermit, his commanding officer, several aristocratic patrons, such patriarchal social institutions as the Inquisition and the University, and finally, but most importantly, his doctors. The satirist betrays the extent to which such figures are both longed for and tenaciously resisted ("I do not love him – I hate him").

Traces of megalomania – witness Torres' endless boasting – are rarely absent from, indeed, may predominate in, a personality strongly inclined to paranoia, in accordance with a process whereby the "liberated libido becomes attached to the ego, and is used for the aggrandizement of the ego." [18] A return is thus made to the stage of narcissism, in which a person's only sexual object is his own dilated ego. There are, for example, strikingly narcissistic tendencies in evidence in Torres' extensive self-portrait and, on a more general scale, in his very utilization of the autobiographical genre. This regression to narcissism, in the case of Torres, is strengthened by delusional ideas of a hypochondriacal nature – we are spared no detail of his physical illness – which culminate in his final break-down, an attack of melancholia, induced in part by a series of personal setbacks and the death of his patron, Cardinal Molina. Although his melancholia alternates with mania – in combination, they account for the ebb and flow of vitality throughout his life – the hypertrophy of his femininity explains his final depression.

Contrary to the layman's expectations, the onset of depression does not herald any withdrawal from reality: the melancholic's self-

---

[16] The "Wolf Man," IX, 225-366 (256).
[17] Freud, "A Child is Being Beaten," X, 159-193 (175).
[18] Freud, "Schreber," 211.

disparagement lacks any sense of shame. As Freud warns: "One might emphasize the presence in him [the melancholic] of an almost opposite trait of insistent communicativeness which finds expression in self-exposure."[19] The autobiography, as a genre, suits Torres' purposes admirably, since it enables him to record every injustice and slight, however minute, and thereby to make a thorough nuisance of himself.

Predictably, Torres rehearses this psychodrama in the very act of writing. He is unable to contain the violence of anal pleasure, which disturbs the capacity for symbolization. This helps explain the very real impression that his texts give of being largely self-referential exercises in sheer auto-erotic, polymorphous self-indulgence. Their *jouissance,* that is to say, is onanistic rather than copulatory. While Torres assures us that, if he wished, he could cease to write, could still this masturbatory hand (230), he obviously finds too much delight in letting the ink flow to desist. Hence the ongoing narcissistic contemplation of his own literary image.

In contrast to the idealist, Torres regresses to a pre-subjective narcissism, grounded in a genuinely material, that is to say, social, historical context. Significantly, social humiliations figure prominently in the etiological circumstances of his paranoia, in particular in the form of the disparagement of his discipline, astrology, by enlightened rationalists. It was not, of course, just his own dirty linen that he was prepared to launder in public. Torres is unbearable because he is a *public* monstrosity. He it was, after all, who proclaimed the pathology of normalcy. Whereas his bourgeois contemporaries were busy locking up their neighbours to assure themselves of their own sanity, the satirist exhibited both his own neurosis and that of his gentlemen friends. He is familiar with the underside of the social organism, the paranoid reality of which polite society is secretly aware but which it prefers not to see. In the context of the Enlightenment his paranoia is the "dark side of cognition" (Adorno and Horkheimer, 195).

By emphasizing his bourgeois characteristics, modern critics have radically misrepresented Torres. The scandal of the Establishment (which now houses these critics), he is intent upon unmasking academic claims to a disinterested quest for truth in all their sordid detail:

---

[19] "Mourning and Melancholia," XI, 245-68 (255).

> A los libros ancianos aún les conservaba algún respeto; pero después que vi que los libros se forjaban en unas cabezas tan achacosas como la mía, acabaron de poseer mi espíritu el desengaño y aborrecimiento. Los libros gordos, los magros, los chicos y los grandes, son unas alhajas que entretienen y sirven en el comercio de los hombres [. . .]. Todos están hechos por hombres y, precisamente, han de ser defectuosos y oscuros como el hombre. Unos los hacen por vanidad, otros por codicia, otros por la solicitud de los aplausos, y es rarísimo el que para el bien público se escribe. Yo soy autor de doce libros, y todos los he escrito con el ansia de ganar dinero para mantenerme. Esto nadie lo quiere confesar; pero atisbemos a todos los hipócritas, melancólicos embusteros que suelen decir en sus prólogos que por el servicio de Dios, el bien del prójimo y redención de las almas dan a luz aquella obra. (115)

Needless to say he reserves his most poisonous arrows for science, and in particular for those bourgeois professionals *par excellence,* the doctors, who, as engineers of health, were also the major planners of society. Hardened by daily encounter with the sick and dying, medical practitioners become the very symbol of social oppression and power for their patient: "Para instruirse en el idioma de la medicina y comer sus aforismos basta un curso cualquiera, y pasan de doce mil los que hay impresos sin más novedad que repetirse, trasladarse y maldecirse los unos a los otros; y lo mismo sucede entre los oficiales y maestros que parlan y practican las demás ciencias" (116). Of course, nobody can knock down the clown himself, since he has already thrown himself to the ground: "Yo confieso que para mí perdieron el crédito y la estimación los libros después que vi que se vendían y apreciaban los míos, siendo hechuras de un hombre loco, absolutamente ignorante y relleno de desvaríos y extrañas inquietudes" (116).

One understands why Borges, along with his fellow bourgeois critics, found it prudent to keep Torres ("hombre impoético" [I, 13]) and his autobiography ("documento insatisfactorio" [I, 9]) at a distance. Whether in light of the "intentional fallacy" or the "death of the author," these critics are at one in insulating the literary work against the influence of the outside world. This insulation is carried over by New Critics into their repudiation of the carnal aspects of affective criticism; and if neo-idealists and post-structuralists have induced a certain amount of panic through the discovery of reader-power, they have had more bark than bite. Revealingly, their "ideal" readers are not located in terms of class, except to the extent that an indulgence, on the part of both reader and critic, in the "pleasure of the text" betrays the hedonism of people with few financial worries.

CHAPTER IV

THE IDEAL REVOLUTION: ROMANTICISM AND ITS LEGACY

I

The assessment of Borges' attitude to Romanticism, and of the impact of this movement on him, concerns an important but problematic aspect of his work. Borges himself refers derisively to the "vocinglero individualismo" of Romanticism (I, 93), thereby highlighting an important aspect of this movement which, in essence, was a reaction against the crisis of the autonomous subject in the second phase of Industrial Capitalism. In the hands of the Romantics, language is rooted not in things perceived, but in the active subject. It involves a process of creation and recreation, embodies a dynamic, regenerative force that does not *represent* (as in classicism) but manifests the will of those that speak it. It is, to use W. von Humboldt's terms, not *ergon* but *energeia,* a spiritual presence which, in a sense, brings *man* into existence as a possible object of thought.[1]

However, Romanticism is contradictory at its core. It begins with a rebellion in the name of the freedom of the individual, and ends with the loss of individuality, in a union with nature. Linguistically, this union equates with a regression to the semiotic. Since individuality is constructed by virtue of entry into the symbolic, to step outside it, into the semiotic, is to relinquish one's very identity. Ultimate freedom, in other words, consists of the extinction of the individual. Symbolic language is the imprisoning factor, but there can be no escape from it, except into the deathly inertia of matter. Hence the final gloom of Romanticism.[2]

---

[1] See Foucault (1970), 288-300.
[2] See Belsey, 118-24; Josipovici, 190-203.

The transparent language of classicism provided no locus from which to construct a "science of man." Its *cogito* institutes a pure, transcendental subject, and a linguistic regime centred on the noun. With Romanticism, a whole mystique is born, that of the verb as the primordial element of speech. The verb is a poetic flash, the crest of a wave that disappears leaving nothing behind – as in the language of Tlön – or almost nothing. Sedimentation is imperceptible but real. An historical tradition is born and preserved in the very texture of speech. Language, in other words, re-acquires some of the localized density that it had possessed in the Renaissance and had lost in the classical period. It becomes again an object of scrutiny, to be peeled away, layer by layer, so as to expose the Truth that lies hidden within.

By the same token, however, the material influx into language destabilizes the subject, which reacts with another wave of rejection. In turn this feeds a process of sublimation, which inflicts upon the subject a sense of non-being. The language of Tlön is, after all, based upon the philosophy of idealism, in terms of which the soma can only ever be an idealized body, and the drive patterns merely the simulacrum of an original motility. The disembodied flux is re-contained within the subject, failing to open out into a genuinely social outside. Given his class formation, the Romantic must finally refuse to recognise that the unconscious knows neither "mine" nor "yours." He cannot afford to relinquish his property, which includes his ego, and at no time is he more tenacious than when defending his linguistic propriety.

This drama of the body, it is apparent, is that of the body politic. Literature confronts *order* at its most fundamental level, namely that of History. Those lonely, unhappy protagonists, such as Asterión, whom Borges would have us accept as the symbols of essential man,[3] are in reality the products of an industrial capitalism which drove the Romantic into the solitariness of his own creative mind, at the same time as it implicated him in the whole process of commodity production.

The independence movement in Latin America, inspired by the example of the French Revolution, evinces all the compromises and betrayals that historically attend such movements. Ideologically, the strains are apparent regarding the crucial area of language. Andrés

---

[3] See Irby *et al.*, 29.

Bello, for example, possibly inspired by the work of W. von Humboldt, emphasized the expressive, irrational and, therefore, subversive element in language, distancing himself in this respect from the universalist grammar of the Enlightenment.[4] Once the political liberation of the Republic had been achieved, however, the conservative bourgeoisie of the old colonial centres, into which Bello was born, moved to break the impetus for change, at which point it appealed to the authority of French rationalism. Coincidentally with his Romantic emphasis on the imagination, Bello reasserts the "ideal," abstract character of language, independent of its material, contextual existence. In practice, of course, his ideal norms are based on the speech of the educated, that is, of his own class.[5]

On the outer fringes of the Empire, in Argentina, the bourgeoisie was more committed to achieving political and economic independence from an imperialist regime that had long been restricting its trading practices. Its provincial attitude found expression linguistically in the greater liberation recommended by D. F. Sarmiento, which brought him into conflict with Bello in the famous polemic of 1842. In Sarmiento, who was president from 1868 till 1874, Romanticism was a progressive force, sufficiently tempered by the rule of law to permit the proper functioning of trade and commerce. Under the banner of "freedom," the miserable collection of Indians of the interior were exterminated, and political power wrested from the rural bosses.[6] Between 1880 and 1900 the liberal oligarchy, to which Borges belongs by birth, reached the peak of its power and influence. The Romantic spirit of progress of a more youthful bourgeoisie is surrendered for a contemplative attitude more typical of classicism: "Un quietismo desdeñoso de la historia como índice de cambio, de suciedad y perturbación y que para reemplazarla va poniendo de su parte [. . .] a la eternidad como clima y región de lo inmutable" (Viñas [1964], 52).

The modern linguistic establishment, that bulwark of conservatism, hastens to lend support to Bello in his battle against an "individualismo discordante, rupturismo lingüístico y falta de conci-

---

[4] See Urrutia, 268, 276-8.
[5] Ibid, 267, 277.
[6] For an excellent analysis of the balance of power in these and subsequent years, see Torcuato S. de Tella's "Stalemate or Coexistence in Argentina," in Petras and Zeitlin (eds), 249-63. For more detail of the Conquest o the Desert, see Viñas (1982).

liación de lo nuevo con lo tradicional en el ámbito de la cultura" (Urrutia, 278-9, 281). Bello refutes Sarmiento "con finura e ironía," through affirmations that "hoy son verdades y lugares comunes." These include the need, politically and linguistically, for a body of wise men to rule society. True to its tradition, the bourgeois academy brazenly presents such claims not as ideological baggage but as "objetividad científica, sin dogmatismos de escuela o doctrina."

II

Borges belonged to a class no longer riding high on the tide of history, to a class whose living space in the city was closing in around it. The public sphere, which had once coincided with its own parameters, had been invaded. The Jockey Club provided an assembly point, from which the bourgeoisie was able to safely contemplate an Other, identified with the "trash," the odorous, pestiferous masses of immigrants proliferating in Buenos Aires.[7] Understandably, the youthful Borges distanced himself from the key Romantic myth of the richness of the Folk. The Romantics, he believed, had erred in contrasting the inflexible verse of learned writers with the richly improvised nature of popular verse. The truth is the reverse: academic verse makes extensive use of new metaphors, unlike popular verse, which is relatively limited in its rhetorical resources. The popular poet deals with universal, public themes ("anchas emociones primordiales" [I, 70]). In contrast the literatus defamiliarizes language in order to express what is unique. Hence his interest in the private ownership of language.

Borges' attitude to Romanticism, however, is nothing if not complex. For in order to rationalize his emphasis on individuality, he appeals to that strand of Romanticism characterized by interiorization. It is the Romantic in Borges that drives him to seek the phenomenonal specificity of the object, as distinct from its abstract generality. For example, he argues that a term such as *higuera* encompasses and abbreviates a whole host of impressions based on the different bodily senses. Whereas the masses have been insensitized to the complexity of life by a medium which "sólo ha efectuado una parte muy chica de las combinaciones infatigables que po-

---

[7] See Viñas (1964), 236.

drían llevarse a cabo" (T, 48), the writer, *qua* Romantic, feels deeply frustrated by the "fatality" of public discourse, "la díscola forzosidad de todo escritor" (I, 67). Any poet worthy of the name must struggle to match the "privacy" of his thoughts with the "publicity" of language (I, 106). His central task is to name the unnamed.

This concrete world that the poet rediscovers – and it would be impossible to overestimate the importance of this point – is remarkably less material than appearances might suggest. Certainly, the poet flees the artifice of the city and society, as the product of rationality, for the natural world in which, perhaps fleetingly, he glimpses life in all its stark mystery and terror. Borges was himself bequeathed such a moment, a mystical vision of eternity, while wandering through the suburbs of Buenos Aires (HE, 37-41). Here, as elsewhere, the sublime preserves the memory of an imaginary union with the mother's body, before the rupture between subject and object. At the same time, however, unity is reconstituted at a higher level, which registers the lack, the pain of the lost object, caused by the paternal "no." The self to which Borges is restored is a disembodied Platonic archetype. It is a phantom who finds immortality not in the primeval inertia of mother earth, but in the etherealized realm of the patriarch.

Romanticism reproduces this paradox in its attitudes to language. For while it breaks with the voiceless letters of classicism, it postulates a body of pure sound that is cleansed of all materiality. The *energeia* embodied in language remains curiously insubstantial: rather than located in a social context, it connects only with ideas about social practice. The "nation," "society," the "individual," and other such categories, do not refer to the reality lived by people in their everyday lives. Above all, the individual is never implicated in terms of class.

The "language" which most answered the Romantic's needs – a natural idiom, which was yet bodiless – was music. Unlike speech, which aspires to mere communication, music aims at and achieves direct communion. By eradicating all referential content, it establishes itself as pure form and remains forever the idealist's image of an Adamic tongue: "[H]e sentido como posiblemente verdadera la sentencia de Pater, según la cual todas las artes aspiran a la condición de la música: *posiblemente,* porque en la música la forma se confunde con el fondo; no podemos vivirla" (Sorrentino, 32).

Borges therefore finds it absurd that words should ever be added to music. He elaborates elsewhere:

> Schopenhauer [. . .] ha escrito que la música no es menos inmediata que el mundo mismo; sin mundo, sin un caudal común de memorias evocables por el lenguaje, no habría, ciertamente, literatura, pero la música prescinde del mundo, podría haber música y no mundo. La música es la voluntad, la pasión; el tango antiguo, como música, suele directamente transmitir esa belicosa alegría cuya expresión verbal ensayaron, en edades remotas, rapsodas griegos y germánicos. (EC, 148-9)

In Schopenhauer Borges discovers the idealist fantasy of transcending subjecthood pressed to its logical conclusion, in which the aesthetic achieves its ultimate goal of unmediated knowledge. The very intensity of his response, however, alerts us to the origins of Will in an aggressive bourgeois order which "serialize[s] all individuals to equal exhangeability" (Eagleton [1990], 168). As Eagleton explains: "It is as though the cool disregard for specific identities displayed by the capitalist mode of production must be dignified by a spiritual discipline, elevated to a tender mutuality of souls" (169).

III

At the summit of its power, between 1890 and 1900, the oligarchy was served by a body of professional writers both directly, in the writers' capacity of pro-establishment journalists, and indirectly, through their aesthetic practice as *modernistas*. As David Viñas comments, the oligarchical heaven may not have been Olympus, but it paid promptly (Viñas [1964], 274). However, the situation of these writers within the ideological state apparatus was not without its contradictions. *Modernismo,* it is true, dematerializes and fetishizes the work of art, which is thereby transformed into one more consumer item, and betrays, through its elitism, a certain arrogance and aggression typical of any dominant imperialist class. At the same time it affirms, through its philosophy of art-for-art's sake, the existence of a realm of authentic experience independent of the "system" and its materialist values. *Modernismo* is, in short, both a product of, and a form of resistance to, the market mentality of capitalism.

It was against *modernismo* that the youthful Borges and his avant-garde colleagues rebelled: "Los preceptistas hablan de lenguaje poético, pero si queremos tenerlo, nos entregan un par de vanidades como corcel y céfiro y purpúreo y don en vez de donde. ¿Qué persuasión de poesía hay en soniditos como ésos? ¿Qué tienen de poéticos?" (T, 48). Drawing moral support from Irigoyen's new radicalism, they called into question the (poetic) values of the oligarchy. Above all, they rejected the *modernista*'s isolation of poetry from everyday life: "Hartos estábamos de la insolencia de palabras y de la musical imprecisión que los poetas del novecientos amaron" (P, 106). This is somewhat indecisive as criticism – a warning perhaps of things to come – but there is no gainsaying the dissatisfaction that it expresses with a poetry all too fragile and effete.

The new generation of poets advocated an *ultraísmo* which, in place of the poetic tradition of their fathers, returned to the Romantic notion of an Adamic tongue. With the presumption of youth, the *ultraísta* would be father-of-himself, on whom devolves the task of naming: "[. . .] fue el anhelo de recabar un arte absoluto [. . .] que durase en la perennidad del idioma [. . .] solicitando un límpido arte que fuese tan intemporal como las estrellas de siempre" (Gertel, 59). Anxiety of influence drove the *ultraístas*, along with their contemporaries, the futurists and surrealists, to subvert patriarchal discourse.[8] The principal instrument of subversion was the metaphor: "La fatigamos largamente y nuestras vigilias fueron asiduas" (I, 27). Needless to say, it is not merely *modernismo* that is at issue but (scientific) positivism, the official philosophy of the bourgeoisie. Amongst other things, the metaphor, by joining the disparate, disturbs "law and order," even if only of the scientific kind: "Dimos con ella y fue el conjuro mediante el cual desordenamos el universo rígido" (I, 27).

Whatever its political potential, Borges' *ultraísmo*, like Irigoyen's government, proved to be rather less radical than it promised. Just as the Radicals failed to live up to their name, so *ultraísmo* instituted a "beyond" not fundamentally different from what had preceded. It constituted a variation of that youthful, anarchic rebelliousness which wanes quickly and shamelessly with the onset of adulthood. Not surprisingly, the oligarchy was prepared to tolerate, even to encourage, the avant-garde (with some anxiety at first), pro-

---

[8] See Running, 29-30.

vided of course that the latter remained within the bounds of literature. In this way the power-base responds to bohemia as ruling classes traditionally respond to any movement that they cannot defeat, by absorbing it.

At the same time, *ultraísmo* fails not merely because of external pressure but because of its own internal contradictions. Principally, the artistic purity to which it lays claim contrasts starkly with the "disorder" that it would inflict upon the world. Revolutions are always of the body, against the head. *Ultraísmo,* through its anal anxieties, demonstrates the avant-garde's ambivalence towards such carnal forms: "Pide a cada poeta una visión desnuda de las cosas, limpia de estigmas ancestrales; una visión fragrante, como si ante sus ojos fuese surgiendo auroralmente el mundo" (Barnatán, 64). The sources of such contradictions, we believe, are ultimately political. The body that *ultraísmo* would liberate from capitalist oppression can only be the body politic. Once the wayward sons of the oligarchy perceive this fact, they experience a wave of revulsion. Faced by the reality of the immigrant masses, the new industrial proletariat which is beginning to clamour for representation, Bohemia loses its nerve and retreats into the idealists' fold.

In the end *ultraísmo* repressed the unconscious that it had discovered, insofar as this was a political unconscious. In consequence, the displacement of the boundaries of a socially established signifying practice entered a blind alley, and became a harmless bonus. Although it dissents from dominant economic and ideological practices, Literature also plays into the hands of the Establishment: through his work, the writer provides the system with what it lacks – rejection – but keeps it in a domain apart, confining it to the inner experience of an elite. The text becomes the agent of a new religion, whose esoteric practices are marked off from any contaminating truck with the real, and, in consequence, are unable to serve as the vehicle of a revolutionary ideology capable of transforming society.

Borges' path away from *modernismo* is revealing of his own ideological compromises. He will be neither public (in the prophetic strain) nor private (like the *modernista*). Rejecting Darío's work as devoid of "substantial content" (I, 153), his interests will focus on "serious" thought, derived from idealist philosophy. He will highlight, however not the intellectual content of this philosophy *per se,* but its aesthetic appeal. The illusion of a positive transcendence has been transformed into its negative counterpart. It is no longer literature's remoteness from everyday life which is deemed objectionable, but the material resonances of its hidden affinities and relationships: "en realidad no hay tales armazones ni recovecos soterraños, y equivócanse de medio a medio los que creen en el alma de las cosas. Las cosas sólo existen en cuanto las advierte nuestra conciencia y no tienen residuo autónomo alguno" (I, 156).

Gradually, the enthusiasm for the metaphor declines. Borges begins to drift towards a position that will see him reverse his earlier judgement on the excellence of metaphorically complex, learned verse (vis-à-vis the simplicity of folk poetry). He will increasingly look to whole systems of thought as metaphorical: "Añadir provincias al ser, alucinar ciudades y espacios de la conjunta realidad, es aventura heroica" (I, 28). If reality as such is not accessible, there can be no limit to our dreams, to the play of our imagination. The childish activity of *ultraísmo* is rejected ("Hemos de rebasar tales juegos" [I, 29]), in favour of a more serious ludic activity: "Hay que manifestar ese antojo hecho forzosa realidad de una mente: hay que mostrar un individuo que se introduce en el cristal y que persiste en su ilusorio país (donde hay figuraciones y colores, pero regidos de inmovible silencio) y que se siente el bochorno de no ser más que un simulacro que obliteran las noches y que las vislumbres permiten" (I, 29).

IV

Although Borges derives his idealism from a variety of sources, which include bourgeois anthropology (e.g., Fraser) and Anglo-Saxon philosophy proper (e.g., Locke, Berkeley, Hume, and Bradley), he was primarily indebted to the neo-idealist movement of the late nineteenth and early twentieth centuries, which in turn had its roots in the classical idealist philosophy of Kant and Hegel. Neo-idealism, which originated in Germany, had as its basic premise the notion that reality lay in the "spirit" or "idea" rather than in the data of sense perception. It was above all anti-positivist, taking positivism in the general sense of the tendency to discuss human behaviour in terms of analogies drawn from the natural sciences.[9]

---

[9] See Lichtheim, 267-9; Passmore, 300-2.

From Germany, neo-idealism passed into Italy, where Croce mounted possibly the most sustained defence of the Hegelian doctrine of the Spirit. Croce opposed any suggestion that there is an entity which lies wholly outside the human spirit. In his work, the rift between subject and object is overcome by assimilating the latter to the former, in an act of expression or intuition. It is through such acts, he believed, and the struggle that they presuppose, that the mind discovers its own recreative capacities. Conceived in this way, the Hegelian dialectic generates a constantly evolving, forever provisional reality, from which language emerges as a dynamic process resistant to all attempts at systematization.

Borges, who exhibited a life-long fascination with the Italian philosopher and aesthetician, summarizes Croce's views and his own reaction to them thus: "Su fórmula [. . .] es la identidad de lo estético y de lo expresivo. No la rechazo, pero quiero observar que los escritores de hábito clásico más bien rehuyen lo expresivo" (D, 67). The appraisal is sound enough, and indicative of Borges' esteem for Croce's brand of neo-idealism, but it also betrays a sense of unease. It is clear that the modernist, in his classical mode, baulked at Croce's wholesale rejection of linguistic categorization, lexical, morphological and grammatical (cf. IA, 15). He perceives as ideologically subversive the ploy to substitute for the paradigmatic stasis of classicism the syntagmatic flow of romanticism. The order of the symbolic was, after all, integral to the stability of bourgeois society, as indeed was the "conventionalist" thesis currently propounded by positivist linguistics. This stability was jeopardized by the idealist's privileging of diachronic change over synchronic ahistoricity, not to mention his refusal of grammar and his "naturalist" faith in the body of language.

Nevertheless, Borges' apprehension was misplaced. Croce's revolutionary zeal was confined to the preconscious (in the Freudian sense of the term): it closes off all negativity within consciousness.[10] In Croce's own words: "La genialità intuitiva o artistica, come ogni forma d'attività umana, è sempre cosciente, altrimenti, sarebbe cieco meccanismo" (Croce, 18). Materialistically conceived, as in contemporary psychoanalysis, the unconscious was a closed world to Croce. By the same token, idealist linguistics was denied a physiological basis; it posits a motility in which language merely mimics

---

[10] See Hughes, 226.

the drive patterns of the unconscious. This disembodied flux finds its most perennial expression in the pure form of music, a condition to which all arts aspire (OI, 12).

Given Borges' allegiance to classicism, literary critics have commonly argued in favour of a break with Crocean idealism.[11] Indications are, however, that such a conclusion is somewhat premature. Certainly, in later years, Borges' ambivalence to the aesthetician remains unchanged: "He leído [. . .] a Croce, sin dificultad alguna" (Irby *et al.,* 94). In *Siete Noches* he is still hedging his bets: "He leído casi todos los libros de Croce y no siempre estoy de acuerdo con él, pero siento su encanto" (13). The identification of literature with expression, Borges insists, is possibly not the profoundest, but it is certainly the least harmful, of critical menoeuvres.

What does emerge from Borges' subsequent treatment, however, is the delicate balance that idealism institutes between the conventionalist and naturalist theses. The rupture between language and the real necessarily favours the former: "Erróneamente, se supone que el lenguaje corresponde a la realidad, a esa cosa tan misteriosa que llamamos la realidad. La verdad es que el lenguaje es otra cosa" (SN, 102). Convention maintains a vital distance between the hegemonic class and the masses that menace it from below. The space that it creates above nature is synonymous with "civilization" itself and with the "freedom" on which the whole bourgeois enterprise rested. At the same time this class also needed to re-integrate those values that had been sacrificed in the interests of economic efficiency. It achieved this through equating literature and language with aesthetics, and covertly throwing the whole naturalist thesis onto a higher level, within the autonomous realm of art. Here, Borges is able to reassess the referential qualities of language, and find poetry superior in this respect to prose. He concludes: "Casi nadie profesa la doctrina de Croce y todos la aplican continuamente" (SN, 102).

Modernism transposes the notion of a poetic object from the word to the total artefact. The latter becomes the vehicle of those "natural," bodily values which are antithetical to patriarchal order: "Tengo para mí que la belleza es una sensación física, algo que sentimos con todo el cuerpo. No es el resultado de un juicio, no llegamos a ella por medio de reglas" (SN, 120). Lacking all social imbri-

---

[11] For example, Sturrock, 87; Alazraki (1974), 159; Rodríguez Monegal (1964).

cation, however, the body is necessarily idealized. The union of subject and object, or reader and writer, is purely mental, achieved through the suppression of the material density of language. The aesthetic (f)act "no requiere ser definido" (SN, 107). Like some mystical encounter, it resists all vulgar, rational scrutiny, and can be experienced only by those with the requisite sensibility: "sentimos la belleza o no la sentimos" (SN, 120). In this private enclave, romantic irrationalism makes its last stand.

V

One of the ingredients in Borges' idealist make-up with which critics have somewhat belatedly engaged is the Argentinian philosopher, Macedonio Fernández. It is an omission for which they have only themselves to blame. For as is his wont, Borges is uncommonly honest and specific in acknowledging his intellectual debt: "Pocas horas le bastaron a Macedonio para convertirnos al idealismo" (P, 49). Macedonio lived idealism with an intensity, to judge from Borges' own account, that few others have managed to equal. In other words, he was committed not merely to a metaphysics but to the practical imperative of the pursuit of perfection. (It is not dialectical materialists alone who have been able to move beyond interpretation to praxis.) This suggests a greater affinity with such Romantic idealists as Schelling rather than with those eminently bourgeois representatives of the enlightenment, the British Empiricists. It was doubtless from this same source that Macedonio also imbibed his sense of cosmic mystery and despair, which he was subsequently to pass on to his youthful disciple.[12]

Macedonio is in many respects the archetypical, alienated victim of industrial capitalism, to the point of parody. Motionless on his bed or sitting in a straight-backed chair, he committed himself totally to the mind: "El cuerpo en él era casi un pretexto para el espíritu" (P, 53). We need to seek the cause of such schizophrenic disintegration in that historical, cultural juncture whereby the aggressive entrepreneur of classical liberalism, bolstered philosophically by Herbert Spencer, has been eclipsed in favour of a passive, interrogative and ultimately inexistent subject. At the same time,

---

[12] See Ferrer, 47-51.

there is no gainsaying the severity of Macedonio's idiosyncratic form of the illness: "Vivía (más que ninguna otra persona que he conocido) para pensar. Diariamente se abandonaba a las vicisitudes y sorpresas del pensamiento, como el nadador a un gran río" (56). Needless to say, this art of inaction presupposes a total estrangement not merely from the individual body but from the body politic. The solitary philosopher finds his natural resting place in a boarding house, that symbol of institutional impersonality *par excellence* in which several of Borges' own short stories are set.

Pursuing the logic of withdrawal, and his commitment to practice, Macedonio attempted to found an anarchist colony in Paraguay. It was a predictable undertaking, given his lack of any political alternative to the dehumanized, bureaucratized form of modern society. For such a beleaguered member of the traditional bourgeoisie, the Romantic drama of escape retains all its attraction and its promise: "En un traspatio de la calle Sarandí, nos dijo una tarde que si él pudiera ir al campo y tenderse al mediodía en la tierra y cerrar los ojos y comprender, distrayéndose de las circunstancias que nos distraen, podría resolver inmediatamente el enigma del mundo" (53). Even within civilization, Macedonio saw the world with a pristine freshness: "Era como si Adán, el primer hombre, pensara y resolviera en el Paraíso los problemas fundamentales" (53).

However, in reality, Macedonio is not a forerunner but a latecomer. Deeply contaminated by idealism, his utopianism was bound to fail, and fail it did, less a solution than a further symptom of capitalist dehumanization. It succumbs to abstraction at the very moment at which it lays claims to the concrete. For in order to see, Macedonio, like his fictional counterpart, Funes, must first close his eyes! And as with any latecomer, in whom repression is excessive, the material world returns with a vengeance. His smile of courtesy and distant air belie a constant fear of pain, quintessentially that inflicted by the dentist, and of death (57), both of which, in their sheer physicality, are the ultimate affront to a creature who would identify himself with the absolute Spirit.

VI

Macedonio Fernández's attempt to flee the city, while very much a Romantic gesture, indicates new developments in Argentinian culture and society. For whereas bourgeois idealists of the Generation of 1837 looked upon Buenos Aires as a beloved or a mother, subsequent generations perceived in her the form of a great whore: "Buenos Aires después del 80 se torna imposible: olores, chimeneas, gringos" (Viñas [1964], 54). The effects of urbanization are a recurrent theme of Borges' fiction. Dahlman, for example, struggles to free himself from the city's clutches: "Se despertó con náuseas [. . .] En esos días, Dahlmann minuciosamente se odió; odió su identidad, sus necesidades corporales, su humillación, la barba que le erizaba la cara" (F, 197). Reduced to his aching body, he is denied the dignity of a spiritual existence: "Las miserias físicas y la incesante previsión de las malas noches no le habían dejado pensar en algo tan abstracto como la muerte" (197). Woman is a bleeding witch who knows only a purely physical mode of existence.

After 1900 the beleaguered bourgeois looked for his models of purity less to Europe, where the proletariat was also mobilizing its forces, than to the Pampas. Needless to say, the reality of the interior – the destruction of the gaucho by the bourgeoisie itself, the nitty-gritty of property rights, the exploitation of labour – was filtered through a haze of idealization: "[. . .] porque su directo conocimiento de la campaña era harto inferior a su conocimiento nostálgico y literario" (200).

Dahlmann returns to his origins: "pudo sospechar que viajaba al pasado y no sólo al Sur" (200). From the dream world of the city, he moves towards "un mundo más antiguo y firme [. . .] No turbaban la tierra elemental ni poblaciones ni otros signos humanos" (198, 200). At the same time, however, the convalescent is in flight from origins. The maternal body that awaits him is a madonna, from whom all carnal life has been repressed: "la larga casa rosada que alguna vez fue carmesí" (196). The impression of spirituality is enhanced by such images as that of the train winding toward the infinite horizon. Borges struggles to capture the sense of paradox: "Todo era vasto, pero al mismo tiempo era íntimo y, de alguna manera, secreto" (200). There was a time, in the womb, when we were the whole universe. Through literature, Dahlmann returns to this time. He demonstrates the truth of the claim that in reading and writing we engage in a copulatory act, which is a uterine regression. The dreamer is split into two, sinks into himself, into a whole new world made out of his own body. "Both the phallic hero and the female space are made out of the one body of the dreamer" (Brown [1966], 51). Simultaneously, the hero is denied such intimacy by a phallic law that reminds him of his smallness: he is a phallus in an empty room, wandering over an open plain that is boxed in by the sky. We are all, we are nothing – a familiar enough experience to self-centred consumers who are yet the decentred victims of capitalist production.

Oligarchal writers like Borges rejuvenate the gaucho as part of a reaction against the urban proletariat who formed the power base of Irigoyen's Radical Party. The ideological role of the plainsman who confronts and eliminates Dahlmann is precisely that of reconciling exemplary status with "lived experience." As exemplar, he is the classical archetype, who stands outside of history, in whom "[la realidad] se va desmaterializando hasta resultar leve, casi incorpórea" (Viñas [1964], 102). His silence and withdrawnness signify an inner reserve, that knows only the cyclic time of myth and the vertiginous depths of the Spirit. Exteriorized in the "eternity of the moment," however, he is flattened out into the urban plebeian whose animal presence inspired such terror in the liberal intellectual. Through his contradictory qualities, this *compadre* constitutes the paradox that awaits any thinker who, in order to grasp the concrete, must first abstract it from its social context. In psychological terms, this same thinker attempts to contain negativity within the confines of consciousness. In this respect, as in others, Borges betrays his debt to Hegelian idealism.[13]

---

[13] Regarding the relationship between the concrete and the abstract, compare Hegels's comment:

> Empiricism [. . .] labours under a delusion, if it supposes that, while analysing the objects, it leaves them as they were: it really transforms the concrete into an abstract. And as a consequence of this change the living thing is killed: life can existe only in the concrete and one (Hegel, 143).

In turn, Marx found Hegel to be guilty of abstraction and of failing to realize that reality for man can only be social:

> The activities and agencies of the state are bound to individuals (the state is effective only through individuals), but not to the individual conceived as a *physical* being, only as a being of the *state;* they are bound to the *state-like qualities* of the individual. It is therefore ridiculous for Hegel to assert that these offices "are linked with particular persons in *an external and contingent way."* On the contrary, they are linked to the individual by a *vinculum substantiale*, by an essential quality in him. They are the natural outcome of that essential quality. The confusion arises because Hegel regards the activities and agencies of the state abstractly, for themselves, as opposed to particular individuality; in doing

VII

Croce's idealism flowed back into Germany, where it rejoined the native tradition, through the philosophical work of Fritz Mauthner (1910), and stimulated Karl Vossler to seek idealist solutions to practical linguistic data. It was developed further by G. Bartoni, M. Bartoli, and other members of a Neolinguistic School. Neo-idealism also dominated Spanish linguistics in both the pre- and post- war periods, through such scholars as Dámaso and Amado Alonso, the latter being particularly instrumental in its transferral to the New World.[14]

Neo-idealist criticism of both neogrammarian and structuralist linguistics centres on the crucial issue of the autonomy of the subject, which was under threat in advanced capitalism. Neogrammarians saw linguistic laws as operating in an irresistible, mechanical manner, on an unconscious level, while Saussure conceived of language ("langue") as a monolithic structure independent of the linguistic activity ("parole") of the individual. In contrast to both, neo-idealists emphasized the part played in language by the *conscious* action of the artist, especially the poet, and the individual in general. They conduct, in short, a rearguard defence of the inventive capacity of the subject, as it found expression in the artesanal stage of production anterior to industrial capitalism. At the same time, however, idealists do not escape the impact of late capitalism. Driven onto the defensive, the creative individual postulated by idealism separates himself from the masses, so as to be able to practice in private his marginalized, minority culture. He leaves unchallenged (and therefore accepts by default) the alienated values of the public sphere.

Borges' own thoughts on language were conditioned by the neo-idealist ambience of the Hispanic cultural world.[15] From the first,

---

so he forgets that particular individuality is a human function and that the activities and agencies of the state are likewise human functions; he forgets that the essence of the "particular person" is not his beard and blood and abstract *Physis,* but his *social quality,* and that the affairs of state are nothing but the modes of action and existence of the social qualities of men (Marx [1975], 77-78).

[14] See Iordan and Orr, chapter 2; Hall; Christmann.
[15] See Hart. Most attempts by literary critics to place Borges in terms of his debt to linguistics have been seriously misleading. Foster attempts to connect Borges di-

grammatical distinctions are "una arbitrariedad que [el idealista] acepta a pesar suyo" (I, 66). Ordinary language is an abstraction, just one way of ordering the buzzing, blooming confusion of the world as it assails our senses. Borges delights in the mise-en-abîme effect produced by the impact of raw experience, in all its diversity, before it is mediated by language, before, that is to say, it is alienated, reified and depersonalized by the culture of consumerism. He seems never to tire of evoking an alternative classification to that imposed by everyday language, listing, for example, the coldness, sharpness, and brilliance of a dagger; the complexity of events subsumed by the one word *anochecer;* a vision of a stormy sky; certain smells; the sight of the wind beating the road; the feeling that a walking-stick gives when grasped in the palm of the hand; not to mention "la sencillez del primer farol albriciando el confiado anochecer" (67). With such pseudo-categories, formalized in his Chinese encyclopedia and subsumed in the Aleph, Borges seeks to demonstrate that, however useful normal language may be in terms of everyday practicality, we need at times to defamiliarize it. A reality estranged reminds us of the provisional nature of our habitual "map" of the outside world, "que nuestra fantasía merecerá olvidar alguna vez" (66). The abstraction of this map, its excess of absence over presence, is the source of the neo-idealist's frustration. He fantasizes about a full word that would fill the minatory lack caused by the loss of a primal object.

Of all people, however, the idealist does not know what he wants. The objects of his desire, after which he lunges obsessively, are temporary resting places. The polymorphously perverse body of childhood is taboo: "Nuestro lenguaje, desde luego, es demasiadamente visivo y táctil" (66). Linguistically and otherwise, civilization depends upon our capacity to free ourselves from its entanglements: "Las palabras abstractas (el vocabulario metafísico, por ejemplo) son una serie de balbucientes metáforas, mal desasidas de la corporeidad" (66-67). To escape the pull of the body, each word has to be raised ("levantado"). Habit weighs down ("entorpece") usage, causes the paths of thought to solidify and become entrenched (106). Raised to the level of mythic consciousness, the flow of phenomena breaks down the spatial discreteness of things,

---

rectly with Saussure, whereas Echavarría (see Echavarría, 104-16) and Franco (see Franco, 66-69) emphasize the influence of Fritz Mauthner.

and the ontological gap between the subject and object is bridged: "con escasa fórmula conjura [Berkeley] los embustes del dualismo y nos descubre que la realidad no es un acertijo lejano, huraño y trabajosamente descifrable, sino una cercanía íntima, fácil y de todos lados abierta" (110). Thus, pursuing the logic of the idealist's argument, we arrive at the solipsism that awaits every idealist, in which closeness is achieved at the cost of the total dissociation of the mind from body. The subject, utterly motionless and consumed by a sense of its own non-being, contemplates a world which is the product of his own fantasy.

VIII

One consequence of Borges' solipsism was the increasing importance that he attached to conventionalism, as when, for example, he ridicules the Spanish Academy's belief in the "expressive" power of words: "Admirar lo expresivo de las palabras (salvo de algunas voces derivativas y otras onomatopéyicas) es como admirarse de que la calle Arenales sea justamente la que se llama Arenales" (T, 43-44). A subtle, albeit important shift is discernible in his essays. Alongside his continued insistence upon each writer's obligation to experiment with language, Borges gives evidence of his personal satisfaction with Spanish in its present form. It is less the referential funcion of words that is at issue, he protests, than their capacity to invent reality: "los sustantivos se los inventamos a la realidad" (45); "La lengua es edificadora de realidades" (47). Language captures the moon not as it is, but as it seems to each of us, who necessarily see it differently.

Gradually, Borges relinquished on one level the founding principle of Romanticism, namely the poet's ability to grasp the other. This led him to turn to a radical reappraisal of the role of the metaphor, which he now insists, in contradistinction to his earlier standpoint, is only one of the many devices of rhetoric, without any privileged status (IA, 55, 59). Moreover, he proceeds, we are bound to ignore the irrelevant etymological resonances inherent in words if we are to communicate effectively. Such semantic overgrowth, like the proliferation of lexical items, serves as a distraction from real thinking, which depends more upon the conceptual resources of the language: "La numerosidad de representaciones es lo que importa, no la de signos" (170). In this respect, the Academy's inane fabrication of synonyms, dead words whose phonetic variation does not affect ideational content, stands opposed to the classical economy of Wilkins' universal language and Racine's prose style. By the same token, Borges is now well-disposed towards the figurative paucity of popular poetry which he had formerly criticised, and which he now finds consonant with his interest in metaphysical systems imaginatively conceived as total metaphors.

However, discussion of the so-called classical style becomes impossibly fragmented and contradictory, under the pressure of ideological demands. The stipulation that only minor departures from standard usage be permitted, "para no entorpecer la circulación total del idioma" (IA, 178), indicates a deepening of social divisions within language. The "universality" that Borges recommends is descriptive of a dialect imposed by a hegemonic class at an international level, which like any such class, portrays its life-ways as "eternal" and "natural." This dialect is defined by its opposition to that of the disenfranchised part of the population ("un dialecto chúcaro y receloso" [170]), which, although marginalized in terms of the public sphere, imposes itself as the "common language" by the sheer force of numbers of its speakers.

A curious situation therefore arises, whereby a class with universal pretensions imposes "representaciones no llevaderas por el habla común" (T, 48). The ideological function of diglossia, we need to remind ourselves, is "to make it difficult or impossible for the ordinary members of the population to have access to, or participate in, the state institutions which have so much power over their lives" (Devonish, 16). The bourgeoisie is emphatic that centralized institutions employ the official language, *their* language. Despite his love of Buenos Aires, captured in his poetry, Borges was at no point in his career an advocate of the local colour beloved of an earlier Romanticism, nor (except in a stylized literary form) of the "culto de lo plebeyo." The citizens of Buenos Aires, he complained, incline "no al español universal, no a la honesta habla criolla de los mayores, sino a una infame jerigonza" (137). From this oligarchical standpoint, the language of the slums ("arrabalero") is simply inconceivable as a literary medium. The much vaunted "richness" of criminal slang masks a conceptual indigence, and, like the picaresque jargon from which it derives historically, cannot be "cleansed" of the matter from which it was formed: "es barro quebradizo que sólo un milagroso alfarero podrá amasar en vasija de eternidad" (142).

The Romantic flight from a city overrun by a proletariat of foreign extraction implies a kind of Manichean vision according to which the spiritualized interior would save the material body politic.[16] The roots of all such agonic conflicts lie in the economic reality of life, and in the dynamics of scarcity that this reality implies. For in a less than ideal world, characterized by endemic shortage, one individual necessarily flourishes at the expense of another. Any such confrontation, however basic the necessities at issue and however universal its constituent features, is enacted in a historical context. The social background of the idealist's nostalgia for nature is that of a class in decline, seeking to re-establish the values of its ancestors: "No precisaron de otros [. . .] Hoy, esa naturalidad se gastó" (IA, 177). The "plain style," as practised by the bourgeoisie in its heyday, serves to hoard energy. It enables the "free" exchange and circulation of information, according to the model of coinage: "Si la superioridad numérica de un idioma no es canjeable en superioridad mental, representativa, ¿a qué envalentonarse de ella?" (175). In contrast, to press the logic of these metaphors, the more recent expressive styles, which indulge the body, are uneconomic; they have brought about the ruin of a class by squandering its resources.

There is a danger, however, in such a straightforward extrapolation from the economic base to the superstructure, insofar as language is a key element in both, and, as such, deeply affected by their asymmetrical relationship. This asymmetry is responsible for the inherent instability of any diglossic situation within capitalism. The performative efficiency of the masses, we saw earlier, is hindered by too great a gap between the standard language and the speech of the proletariat. The new industrial bourgeoisie of Buenos Aires realized that a basic literacy was required by those entering the industrial work-force, and that this literacy could only be achieved by a more flexible language policy.[17] Even Borges accepted in his early work the distinctive nuances of Argentinian Spanish (IA, 178), and accepted with equanimity the influx into standard

---

[16] See Viñas (1964), 247.
[17] Cf. Entwistle, 254-5, 271-7. For the linguistic complexities of Borges' family background, see Rodríguez Monegal, 17-18.

speech of substandard forms. The latter, he believed, could in no way amount to a destabilizing influence (T, 139). At the same time, any move to liberalize usage arouses anxieties within the hegemonic group, which realizes the ideological importance of language in the maintenance of the relations of production. This explains why the old oligarchy, to which Borges belonged, generally baulked at the prospect of incorporating elements of *porteño* and *lunfardo* into standard Spanish, not to mention the vulgarisms with which the Academy was currently weighing down ("cargando") the Spirit of Spanish. It was particularly eager to reaffirm its "universal" norms at a time when, as a class, it was seriously under threat. Subsequently, Borges even lamented the concession to diversity indicated by the very title of his early work, *El idioma de los argentinos*.[18]

The internal contradictions within the oligarchy are reproduced within literature, hence the strange combination of neo-classicism with a residual romanticism. For once language's referential relationship with reality is broken, the classical *status quo* is subverted from within by the return of "expression." Literature encapsulates an experience of what language can never grasp, without annihilating its own symbloic form. It embodies what can never be known rationally, the semiotic drives that pulsate beneath the fixed structures of patriarchal syntax. The writer depends upon the drives' Dionysian force just as the bourgeoisie depends upon the telluric energy of what it quaintly and euphemistically refers to as the "people." Accordingly, it is to Borges' fictions that we must turn, in order to pursue the politics of idealism to its logical conclusion.

IX

Neo-idealism attempts to contextualize language, but can only generate *ideas* about social context. It is itself of course unable to know the ideological impasse in which it finds itself, which it projects as a universal, existential problem. This is apparent from the fictionalization of the neo-idealist position in "La busca de Averroes," in which Borges explores the problem of the distance between the sign and its referent. Not only is Averroes, Aristotle's commentator, separated from Aristotle's cultural context by four-

---

[18] See Sorrentino, 26, 89.

teen centuries but he is working from a translation of a translation of the original Greek text. Not surprisingly, he is unable to gloss the concepts of "tragedy" and "comedy," though relevant contexts lie close to hand.[19] This experience predictably persuades him of the correctness of the conventionalist thesis: "el idioma y los signos y la escritura son obra de los hombres" (A, 98). There can be no ready access to the world of nature.

Albucásim faces a similar problem when called upon to relate the exotic aspects of his trip to China: "La maravilla es acaso incomunicable; la luna de Bengala no es igual a la luna del Yemen, pero se deja describir con las mismas voces" (98). Like a good naturalist, he seeks to possess the earth again in a primordial immediacy of contact, and succeeds, in spite of language's inalienable generality, in recreating his experience of a theatrical performance. Yet such is the specificity of Albulcásim's description that Averroes fails to recognise its relevance to his own preoccupations. It is a failure that jeopardizes his own identity. Lacking any social context of his own, he teeters on the brink of extinction: "se supo envejecido, inútil, irreal" (99). True to his insubstantiality, he proceeds, in the ensuing literary discussion, to reject both traditional poetry (*modernismo?*) and new avant-garde verse (*ultraísmo?*), in favour of the classical language of the deserts, whose characteristic solipsism manifests itself in the economic use of metaphor.

Pursuing the logic of his conventionalism, Borges must finally step outside of literature, in which, momentarily, he has recaptured a unified experience, facilitated by an unarbitrary language. Reluctantly perhaps, but predictably, ironic man deconstructs the illusion of all fiction. He is as little able to contextualize Averroes as Averroes was able to contextualize Aristotle. The search for Averroes must fail as surely as Averroes's search, and with them the utopia of an Adamic language. The skill, or desperation, of the modernist writer, however, is such that he is able to snatch victory from the jaws of defeat. For in the very practice of his art, he succeeds in *doing* what he cannot *say*, by catching the subject in the act of being. Necessarily, this is achieved at the cost of unleashing an infinite process of regression in which, notwithstanding its mythic disguise, we readily recognise the disembodied nightmare that is the historically localized (un)reality of industrial capitalism.

---

[19] Averroes is also impeded by the fact that Islam forbids the artistic representation of the human figure.

CHAPTER V

TO HAVE AND HAVE NOT: MODERNIST LITERATURE AS FETISHISM

I

Critics have been accustomed to emphasize the subjective integrity of Borges in the early part of his career: "En ese período, la psique y la mente, la intuición de la lógica, la pasión y la razón aún no se habían disociado en Borges y se daban en perfecta hipóstasis, por lo que acentuaba y producía unilateralmente, sin doblez ni dicotomía, en plena entidad vital" (Ferrer, 63). The Romantic poet, safely ensconced within the warmth and intimacy of the maternal home, keeps the debased social world at a distance. The poem itself operates as a mysterious organic unity, in contrast to the fragmented individualism of the capitalist market-place.

However, the self-assertive individualism of the first Romanticism, of which Borges himself complained, had always demonstrated a fundamental weakness; the poet relinquished the alienated world of capitalism for the intensely charged confines of poetry only to discover within the domain of its privacy a central absence. The split between the private and public selves is precisely that: a split. Withdrawn from social implication, the poet voices not Adamic truths but platitudes.[1] The realm of freedom shrinks alarmingly as society becomes even more bureaucratized. The human body is measured, weighed, cured, cared for, and categorized by technicists who scrutinize its every move. An ego that once embraced the whole universe has now shrunk to almost nothingness:

---

[1] See Josipovici, 195-6.

> I offer you that kernel of myself that I have saved, somehow – the central heart that deals not in words, traffics not with dreams, and is untouched by time, by joy, by adversities. (OP, 123)

The final stages of this process of personal disintegration assume, in Borges, the proportions of a mystical experience: "Me sentí muerto, me sentí percibidor abstracto del mundo" (HE, 40). At a moment of revelation, coinciding with his death, the individual catches a glimpse of the totality of things, but, unable to convey this insight through ordinary language, is reduced to silence.

The reality of this Platonic experience, which will find a responsive echo in many people, lies less in its particularity as a unique event, which occurred at night and involved the withdrawal of libidinal contact from the circumambient world, than in its historical, social specificity as a class experience. As such, it is overdetermined. The veil can be lifted only outside of the "normal" time of mechanized, alienated labour, in accordance with a revitalized, archaic sense of reality. Simultaneously, the passive gaze of the mystic is that of the consumer, the dissipation of whose subjective integrity is but one symptom of alienation caused by an oppressively instrumentalized mode of existence. Locked inside the symbolic, although withdrawn from the public sphere, the idealist sensed only his non-existence: "Pienso probar que la personalidad es una trasoñación" (I, 84). The ego, that last bit of private property, has been eclipsed by forces which completely transcend the individual. We are invaded and manipulated by hidden persuaders: "Equivócase quien define la identidad personal como la posesión privativa de algún erario de recuerdos" (85). Needless to say, this crumbling of identity can find no support in the body, dispensed with at a preliminary stage of idealism: "no soy mi actividad de ver, de oír, de oler, de gustar, de palpar. Tampoco soy mi cuerpo, que es fenómeno entre otros" (95).

To the extent that identity survives, it can only be in the form of a public persona, in Borges' case the author of his fictions. "Borges y yo" explores the process whereby this persona usurps the "real," private self. The latter seems to haemorrhage under pressure, leading to a gradual seepage of being (H, 69-70). Borges realizes finally the extent to which, as a man, he has been surpassed.[2] By defini-

---
[2] See Ferrer, 77.

tion, however, this persona which is the public self is a mask, whose own stability is as precariously poised as its interiorized double, and, as we shall see, subject to the same invasion and distortion by the market economy.

II

In a manner reminiscent of Harold Bloom,[3] Borges rewrites literary history in terms of Oedipal conflicts, the effect of which is to emphasize not the release of the unconscious but the continuing repression of its contents. His protagonists are often thinly disguised authors. Recabarren, for example, lives in the shadow of his predecessor, José Hernández, who oppresses him as a father oppresses his son. Arriving late upon the scene of the crime, he is awash with the body of tradition, paralysed in his right (writing) side: "Miró sin lástima su gran cuerpo inútil" (F, 183). The strong poet, and Recabarren is no less, accepts the fact of his belatedness and sets about undermining his predecessor by systematically remoulding or mis-reading his work.[4] Thus he recasts the plot of *Martín Fierro* so as to put to death Hernández's protagonist and thereby to free the voice of his own hero.

Writers, critics, and readers, we suggested in our Introduction, act out a family romance, in accordance with their infinitely permutable roles. Readers, we also remember, never figure prominently as such: they are absorbed by an author whose works boast a perfection which is beyond the reach of any merely worldly criticism. Although incorporated, however, the reader survives in Borges, who, in his capacity as writer, is also the true reader not only of his own but of others' works. For to write is to criticize by rewriting the work of one's predecessor, and to rewrite presupposes an initial re-reading, further to which the neo-idealist will emphasize the reader's (and to a lesser extent the listener's) inventive capacity, as an inalienable part of the recreative process. The neo-idealist emphasis is to the point, and a significant addition. It helps to explain, for example, how Pierre Menard, by virtue of his belatedness, is able to surpass Cervantes: "El texto de Cervantes y el de Menard

---

[3] Cf. Bloom (1973), especially 99 ff.
[4] Cf. Bloom (1975[i]).

son verbalmente idénticos, pero el segundo es casi infinitamente más rico" (F, 56-57).[5]

In the encounter between Fathers and Sons, what is the role of Mothers and Daughters? The question, as Emma Zunz knew, is more than of academic interest.[6] Marginalized within a patriarchal society, we would expect her enthusiasm for phallic encounters to be qualified. And sure enough, at crucial moments she wavers in her support for her father: "recordó (trató de recordar) a su madre" (A, 62). If the construction of any narrative involves a cost, in terms of the ejection of unwanted matter, Emma bears that cost twice over: "Pensó (no pudo no pensar) que su padre le había hecho a su madre la cosa horrible que a ella ahora le hacían" (65). Sexually exploited (and exploiting), she can know, as no man can, what it is to be reduced to a body: "El temor se perdió en la tristeza de su cuerpo, en el asco" (65). At the same time, Emma must battle over the phallus, to the extent that it is the symbol of fullness; and it is as Emma Zunz and not as a mere appendage to her father that she inflicts upon Loewenthal a symbolic castration.

The modernist writer is the biggest woman of all. In the battle with the father, he does not envisage a victory. Gone is the ambition of the first Romantic, and even of the Renaissance humanist who proclaimed the superiority of the Moderns over the Ancients. The phallic, self-assertive subject of classical liberalism can no longer be sustained. The modernist belongs to a class that has run its historical course. In his passivity, manipulated by forces outside of his control, he feels only a sense of non-being.

Accordingly, it is increasingly the formative influence of the past that Borges will emphasize. Like Bloom,[7] he adopts the viewpoint of a writer confronted by the overwhelming presence of the Scriptures. Of course, the instincts of rebellion remain: Otálora "[r]esuelve suplantar, lentamente, a Azevedo Bandeira" (A, 34). And initially the son meets with success: as he waxes, proportionally the greying, ailing father-figure is reduced to the status of a mere reflection. But finally Otálora is denied the objects of his desire, the horse (phallus) and the woman (mother), "adjetivos de un hombre que él aspira a destruir" (34). Engaged in a battle with his pre-

---

[5] See Burgin, 22.
[6] See Brodski, 339, 343-4.
[7] See Bloom (1975[ii]).

cursor – significantly Bandeira receives Otálora "[e]n una suerte de escritorio" (31) – the author finds himself encompassed by another's fiction.

In this way post-modernism would punish us for our incestuous desires, guiding us from the imaginary fullness of the semiotic to the mature responsibility of the symbolic, with its acceptance of lack. It will, in the process, reconcile us to that capitalist alienation whereby the worker confronts his own reified body in the oppressive products of his labour, whose formal richness corresponds with his own inner poverty. Such reconciliation, however, presupposes a number of intermediary stages, at which this same post-modernism will rediscover the imaginary fullness that it appears to relinquish in the Battle of the Authors. The author's incorporation into the body of tradition signals the first instance of the return of the repressed, which we must now consider.

III

The private individual of subjective Romanticism breaks away from the literary work, which accordingly ceases to be "expressive" of an individual consciousness which precedes it. The reader encounters only a fictional construct, the author, who is not to be identified with a human personality, a man of flesh and blood. Accordingly, while this author inherits some of the ambition of the "free," autonomous subject, by not only assimilating but also bettering his predecessors, necessarily he suffers a loss of status, comparable to the withdrawal of the ego. He is not so much an active agent as an insubstantial dream, less the source of meaning than the accident of a tradition working through him. Even the poet, obsessed as he is with origins, arrives late upon the scene of writing: "Every young poet thinks of himself as Adam, naming things. The truth is that he is not Adam and that he has a long tradition behind him. That tradition is the language he is writing in and the literature he has read" (Giovanni *et al.*, 93). For the mature Borges, writing is less creative than recreative. To be original is to innovate within the framework of tradition, like the medieval bard, or to read old texts in new ways, like the cabbalist hermeneutist.

Closer scrutiny, however, suggests that such traditionalism is more apparent than real, or at least, that it springs from a conjuncture of cultural forces historically located in the modern world. For if Borges anticipates a time when everything that can be written is written, that is to say, when to speak is perforce to quote, the anonymity that he celebrates is characteristic not so much of the collective organicism of the primal commune as of a profoundly fragmented and dispersed post-industrial society, in which the citizen has no need of love or friendship, and his favourite pastime is a solitary game of chess (LA, 129). Even in its modernist guise, moreover, self-effacement proves difficult to accommodate. Amongst critics, old habits die hard. For them, originality is health, influence disease. Unable to ignore the sheer presence of tradition in Borges, they interpret his confession of debts as a demonstration of learning, as an example of realism and honesty, and claim such "borrowings" to be, after all, general practice amongst writers. But, when all is said and done, only minor poets cravenly acknowledge their sources. Somehow greatness must be salvaged: "La valentía estilística radica en que Borges osa delatar explícitamente como *no* suyo, algo que, inventado o prestado, le pertenece, por inclusión en su estilo, con idéntica legitimidad que no lo impreso entre comillas" (Tamayo and Ruiz-Díaz, 22).

Even more astray go those critics who have sought to present Borges as a pure classicist. By relinquishing his "personality" for the impersonality of tradition, the idealist escapes not from the self but further into the self. However disembodied and purged of its form, a free-floating modernism remains recognizably the product of the unconscious. Equally, while it is not subjective, neither is it *public;* and if it gives some prominence to ideas, it does so not for their intellectual value *per se.*[8] Gone, it is true, is the self-assertive propheticism of an earlier Romanticism, but what remains, quintessentially the reliance upon a spontaneous "imagination" and "inspiration," derives directly from Romanticism: "Regresemos, pues, a la secular doctrina de que el poeta es un amanuense del Espíritu o de la Musa. La mitología moderna, menos hermosa, opta por recurrir a la Subsconsciencia o aun a lo Subconsciente" (P, 137).

Extending the terms of the debate, we conclude that it is time the displacement of the author, whether through the New Critical "intentional fallacy" or Structuralism's "death of the author," was inspected for its ideological credentials. The separation of the au-

---

[8] See Stead, 34-35, 119-131, and passim.

thor from his works is, after all, merely one more version of the rift between subject and object, which, in turn, corresponds with the process of alienation under capitalism. Just as the worker finds himself confronted by the reified, estranged products of his own labour, so the modernist sees his works as belonging not to himself but to others.

IV

The fragmented identity of the author is recuperated within the text in several ways. One is struck, for example, by the prevalence of autobiographical elements in Borges' work, including the constant preoccupation with his own ancestors, his own direct participation as narrator, the importance attributed in both his fictional and non-fictional writing to literature that he himself has read, and indeed the self-reflexive obsession with literary composition. More importantly, however, authorial unity is retrieved through the figure of the protagonist. This authorian *alter ego,* while it possesses the apparent fullness of a mirror image, belongs to the symbolic. It is a Platonic archetype, and, as such, is structured on the basis of abstraction. Like all archetypes, the protagonist knows no becoming. His biography consists of a mystical moment when he accedes to his quintessential identity: "Imaginemos, *sub specie aeternitatis,* a Droctulft no al individuo Droctulft, que sin duda fue único e insondable (todos los individuos lo son), sino al tipo genérico que de él y de otros muchos como él ha hecho la tradición, que es obra del olvido y de la memoria" (A, 50). Droctulft's vision occurs within sight of Ravenna, the eternal city: he journeys from barbarism to civilization. The preferences of the bourgeois classicist will always lie with the latter. Only for the romantic, who flees its industrial squalor, are Droctulft and the Captive two sides of the same coin.

The classicist is repulsed by the sheer complexity of everyday life, is instinctively offended by the inalienable otherness of those with whom he is most intimate. He raises the world, in the form of language, above its constitutive ambiguity, into the realm of pure spiritual meaning. Such abstraction is achieved by filtering out situational specificities. As Tamayo and Ruiz-Díaz explain in relation to Borges' protagonist Tadeo Isidoro Cruz: "La palabra rescata de cada existencia su recóndita chispa simbólica que permanecía enturbiada, simulada, por la aleatoria multiplicidad circunstancial que el existir concreto impone" (22).

Platonic idealization remains, as always, a basically political gesture, appropriate to a class which, having known its progressive moment in the nineteenth century, is now being swept to destruction: "Fierro cuenta su historia, a partir de la plena edad viril, tiempo en que el hombre *es,* no dócil tiempo en que lo está buscando la vida" (D, 35). The most appropriate genre for a class riding high on the tide of history is the novel, the classic bourgeois genre, which traces the ontogenetic development of an individual character. In contrast, a class that seeks to raise itself above this tide has recourse to a Platonic form which explores those spiritual, eternal qualities of the gaucho. In gaucho poetry the oligarchy celebrates a Mother Earth which it abstracts from all historical implication, and whose brooding silence is eloquent of an inner reserve.[9]

Although even Borges was obliged to admit that Hernández himself pursued a political cause in his work – the defence of the gaucho against metropolitan oppression – he immediately set out to obscure *Martín Fierro*'s ideological resonances. As a good idealist, he was quite prepared to denigrate and place under erasure any reality that proved an obstacle to the higher claims of art. And so he proceeds to applaud Fierro's archetypal victory over his more materialist opponent, the author: "Felizmente, Martín Fierro se impuso a José Hernández [. . .] Yo diría que la voz del protagonista se impuso a los fines circunstanciales del escritor" (P, 93).

In this confrontation, Borges enacts one more version of his favourite theme, the agon, involving this time not two (proto)agonists internal to his fiction, but the author and his protagonist. The setting of this political defeat is that of a number of Borges' short stories: the lonely hotel room, symbol of social alienation and displacement under capitalism. In such a setting Yarmolinsky and Villari met their fate, the real-life Macedonio Fernández whiled away his days, and the solitary Hernández, while composing his masterpiece, was overwhelmed by an invented character who was initially merely an apt rhyme.

At the summit of classical sublimation, however, the repressed returns. This repressed is the source of Borges' enduring Romanticism. The weakening of the patriarchal authority of the author lib-

---

[9] Cf. Ludmer; Prieto.

erates the work's unconscious. (Conscious) intentions count for little. When Borges applauds the victory of Martín Fierro, he signals the resurgence of the Imagination as a force to be reckoned with: "Todo poema que no sea un mecanismo verbal supera lo que se propuso el poeta; la antigua invocación a la Musa no era una fórmula retórica. De ahí lo vano de la poesía comprometida, que niega esa divina y honda raíz y presupone que un poema depende de la voluntad del poeta" (P, 98).

By the same token, this "return" is carefully circumscribed by the boundaries of the text. We can never sufficiently emphasize that Platonization corresponds with a process of political obfuscation. For Borges, conscious intention is the natural domain of ideological commitment. He is unable to see the profoundly "engaged" nature of his own intuitive aestheticism. Clearly, if, as Borges claims, Hernández hid his bourgeois origins very well, the same cannot be said of himself.

V

The opposition between author (Hernández) and protagonist (Martín Fierro) corresponds directly with that other dichotomy involving nature and convention, which is of such momentous importance in Western attitudes to language. *Martín Fierro,* in Borges' view, must be protected against those students of literature that would see the epic as *natural* and would accordingly criticize gaucho poems in realistic terms. Such critics, he argues, suffer from fundamental misconceptions concerning the nature of art: "olvidan que todo arte es convencional" (D, 23). The poet addresses himself not to the real but to the essential, in the Platonic sense of this term: "No pertenece el *Fausto* a la realidad argentina, pertenece – como el tango, como el truco, como Irigoyen – a la mitología argentina" (24). In order to rise to such philosophical heights, gaucho poetry must relinquish the material context, epitomized by the importance attributed to local colour (D, 154). After all, there is no mention of camels in the Koran, the supreme example of the archetypal text.

Emphatically, Borges rejects the prelapsarian view that attributes to South Americans an Adamic status. His insistence on art's conventionality places the gaucho epic at the other end of the tunnel of time: Argentinians are late-comers, an off-shoot of the Greco-Roman tradition of Western Europe. But it is not merely the status of the epic that is at issue. Aesthetic autonomy, it is argued, is an inalienable basis of other genres and styles: "todo arte, aun el naturalista, es convencional y [. . .] las convenciones de aceptación más fácil son las que pertenecen al planteo mismo de las obras" (P, 29). The appeal to Victorian aestheticism in support of such a view confirms the suspicion that what this autonomy holds at bay is the rigidly deterministic operation of natural forces that positivism has stripped of all spiritual essence. The prospective novelist contemplates with a sense of horror the burdensome intrusion of empirical phenomena into the work of art: a total description of the corner of the table upon which he is writing soon extends to two hundred and eleven pages (BD, 21-28). Modernism breaks with such sheer contingency. Briefly Ramón Bonaventa charts its course: the rejection of the real world through the omission of actual names, the privatization of individual lives, and the fragmentation of that bedrock of security, the transcendental ego.

At the same time, however, prelapsarian nature is reconstituted at a higher level. Borges invites us to treat fiction as the Cabbalists treated the Bible and the Universe, that is, as a system cleansed of "noise" and whose elements are, in consequence, all meaningful: "[una novela] debe ser un juego preciso de vigilancias, ecos y afinidades. Todo episodio, en un cuidadoso relato, es de proyección ulterior" (D, 89-90). As always the naturalist exhibits a fascination with those magical qualities that characterize the savage mind. In literature, not only the dead man and the bullet but also the dead man and the wax effigy are bound in a causal relationship (89); the mere mention of a feared event can bring it about ("Larga repercusión tienen las palabras" [90]), in accordance with a "theology" of words and episodes which tolerates no element of chance or redundancy.

In sum, modernist art is distinguished by a dual gesture: it is both conservatively ideological and progressively utopian at the same time. It is ideological insofar as its idealization of experience represents a flight from political reality; stripped of their material context, words are bodiless phantoms, deprived of their sensual magic and the dialogic complexity that characterizes their use by classed speakers in specific situations. It is utopian insofar as it holds up an image, however disembodied, of an "ideal" society; in a world awash with words debased by over-use and commercialization, post-modernism restores to language some of its former power; it asks us to read with heightened awareness, in the belief that only in this way can literature transport us to a level of genuine experience.

VI

The neo-idealist view of language perfectly reflects the Faustian restlessness of man in history. The speaker's urge to close the gap between the sign and its referent is the demand for satisfaction, a demand which can never be met, since the speaker is unconscious of his/her real desires. All such desires are historically based. Teodelina Villar, for example, moulds herself to the demands of a consumer market: "las normas de su credo no eran eternas, sino que se plegaban a los azares de París o de Hollywood" (A, 106). In the radiant surface of her aural form, the buyer sees his own specular shape, and experiences again, however briefly, the fullness of the imaginary.

Language seeks to return to its sources, in the gestures of the Body, but the murder of the soma was the condition of its making, and it must in the last instance swerve away from its object. Hence the endless shifts of fashion: "Teodelina Villar se mostraba en lugares ortodoxos, a la hora ortodoxa, con atributos ortodoxos, pero el desgano, los atributos, la hora y los lugares caducaban casi inmediatamente y servirían (en boca de Teodelina Villar) para definición de lo cursi. Buscaba lo absoluto, como Flaubert, pero lo absoluto en lo momentáneo" (106). Yesterday's fashions (like yesterday's personas) are cast off, in the headlong pursuit of novelty. This pursuit involves, within the idealist scheme of things, an ever-increasing departure from material reality: "Ensayaba continuas metamorfosis, como para huir de sí misma; el color de su pelo y las formas de su peinado eran famosamente inestables. También cambiaban la sonrisa, la tez, el sesgo de los ojos. Desde 1932, *fue estudiosamente delgada* . . ." (106-7, my italics).

As with any bourgeois, Teodelina's mana depends upon her ability to convince others of her "natural," "universal" status. This status is menaced when the public perceives it to be the mere product of history and circumstance. Fittingly, Teodelina's pretensions are exposed by the consumerism of which she is an agent, when a foreign designer off-loads onto her a number of bizarre creations: "al año, se propaló que esos adefesios *nunca se habían llevado en París* y por consiguiente no eran sombreros, sino arbitrarios y desautorizados caprichos" (107). Teodelina's fate is that of the bourgeoisie in general: hit by inflation, her family is one of many that sink into the yawning maw of poverty. Only in death, when the form is freed from its materiality, can Teodelina accede to archetypal status: "sus rasgos recobraron la autoridad que dan la soberbia, el dinero, la juventud, la conciencia de coronar una jerarquía" (107-8).

We move from the world of contingency to the Zahir, which, needless to say, is none other than the commodified work of art itself. In such an aesthetic representation, we behold an auratic object which, in contrast to Teodelina's debased, commodified form, promises to be adequate to our desire. In its very capacity to reflect our gaze, however, this same object evinces the desensualized spirituality which is the hallmark of the Platonic archetype. Like all such archetypes, it expresses the triumph of the paradigmatic over the syntagmatic, in the light of which we come to understand why Borges should write short stories in preference to novels. Texts are honed until they are reduced to a few pages or even a few sentences. Sometimes, as in "El Zahir," he recounts within one story the skeleton plot of another, an essential tale of agonic conflict, of Oedipal strife and anal violence. Such narrative structures stand opposed to the inert resistance of matter: "casi feliz, pensé que nada hay menos material que el dinero [. . .] El dinero es abstracto" (109). Through them, we experience a sense of the freedom that is denied us in the nightmarish world of capitalism: "una moneda simboliza nuestro libre albedrío" (110). Money is the supreme fetish. It serves the solitary writer's narcissistic desires by sublimating his impotence to the point at which it is transformed into omnipotence. With money, we can buy anything, including immortality. The writer will die but his texts will live on.

But at the moment of victory the idealist discovers a paradox; money is the very essence of consumerism. A further paradox follows: the modernist work becomes a mirror image of its opponent, with all its weaknesses, "in a kind of point by point correlation" (Jameson [1971], 35). In the drive towards total organization, Borges apes the socio-economic organization of the proto-fascist societies that he claimed to abhor. His total control as an artist over the last remnants of a refractory contingency shows how contradictions re-enter fiction microcosmically.

Accordingly, while the Zahir liberates the narrator, it also imprisons him: he is a man "possessed." To return to the sanity of everyday language, he must learn to sleep, in other words, to forget the endless nuances that overwhelm us on the level of the particular.

VII

The first Romantic escapes the degrading publicity of language (under capitalism) by retreating into his private inner world. In the process he strips language of its phonetic body:

> Ya se practica la lectura en silencio, síntoma venturoso. Ya hay lector callado de versos. De esa capacidad sigilosa a una escritura puramente ideográfica – directa comunicación de experiencias, no de sonido – hay una distancia incansable, pero siempre menos dilatada que el porvenir.
>
> Releo estas negaciones y pienso: Ignoro si la música sabe desesperar de la música y si el mármol del mármol, pero la literatura es un arte que sabe profetizar aquel tiempo en que habrá enmudecido, y encarnizarse con la propia virtud y enamorarse de la propia disolución y cortejar su fin. (D, 49-50)

It is apparent, however, that the nature rediscovered in such close proximity to music involves extreme sublimation. Language is able to merge with its object for the simple reason that, in its material form, it has ceased to exist. Words, that is to say, have surrendered their referential role, in order to take on independent meaning.

The cost of such measures is soon apparent. In his seclusion, the Romantic idealist discovers that phonetics, for all its materiality, is an absolutely crucial element in language, and that the social context of speech plays a similarly indispensable role: "Nosotros, los que procuramos la paradoja de comunicarnos con los demás por solas palabras – y esas acostadas en un papel – sabemos bien las vergüenzas de nuestro idioma." Even so-called paralinguistic phenomena, the virtues of Romantic solitude notwithstanding, prove far less parasitic upon verbal components that might at first sight seem to be the case: "Nosotros, los renunciadores a ese gran diálogo auxiliar de miradas, de ademanes y de sonrisas, que es la mitad de una conversación y más de la mitad de su encanto, hemos padecido en pobreza propia lo balbuciente que es" (IA, 181-2). Slowly, the realization dawns that language belongs by definition to the public sphere, and that the dream of an authentic, Adamic language, in which words express things in all their uniqueness, can never be more than a Utopian aspiration: "Sabemos que no el desocupado jardinero Adán, sino el diablo – esa pifiadora culebra, ese inventor de la equivocación y de la ventura, ese carozo del azar, ese eclipse de ángel – fue el que bautizó las cosas del mundo" (182).

In contrast to the romantic, the classicist extricates himself from the webs of language by embedding himself firmly within the symbolic. Here, language is "detextualized," in such a way that thoughts correspond perfectly with words. In short, language is equated with speech, in accordance with the phonocentric bias that deconstructionists have repeatedly exposed: "El hecho de una retórica que se interpone es desgraciadamente frecuente. La retórica debería ser un puente, un camino; a veces es una muralla, un obstáculo" (SN, 18). Borges reminds us that the most influential figures in the history of mankind, for example, Pythagoras, the Buddha, Socrates, and Christ, preferred the spoken to the written word. Significantly, one of his own mentors, Macedonio Fernández, scorned writing to the extent that he actually published very little. The stylistic consequences of such phonocentrism are largely predictable: canonic status is accorded to classical writers like Cervantes, at the expense of *modernistas* and of the *culteranistas* and *conceptistas* of the Golden Age. Raised above the flow of history, the art of plain speaking unites the ages in a kind of universal presence.

Even more than the romantic, however, the classicist is plagued by the return of the repressed. The most obvious symptom is a preoccupation with paralinguistic behaviour, without which the words of great men such as Henríquez Ureña, when transcribed, suffer a loss of life: "Ideas que están muertas en el papel fueron alentadoras y vívidas para quienes las escucharon y conservaron, porque detrás de ellas, y en torno de ellas, había un hombre. Aquel hombre y su realidad las bañaban. Una entonación, un gesto, una cara, les daban una virtud que hoy hemos perdido" (P, 84-85). The logic of such a view compels Borges to revise, although only by implication, his earlier estimate of the virtues of silent reading. He reminds us in his mature work that verse originated in song and, in consequence, is still only effective if read aloud (SN, 14).

This renewed emphasis on the phonetic body presages the pervasive resurgence of *jouissance,* the effect of which is to splinter the text, both semantically and syntactically. Such semiotic practice presupposes not the Platonic denigration of print but rather, as Borges' "Del culto de los libros" demonstrates, the converse, namely its sanctification through a process of interiorization (OI, 157-63).[10] The author of *El Aleph* and *Ficciones* is the literator *par excellence,* an archeologist of the written word, who unearths his themes in libraries, archives, and catalogues. His preferred literary model, the Cabbalist, treats the world as a *book,* whose multilayered, intricately allusive content could not be further from the spontaneous availability of oral messages.[11] Indeed, the Cabbalist tradition argues the (chrono)logical precedence of writing over speech. It is in the light of this tradition that Borges erects an alternative literary canon, whose classic texts, by the likes of Flaubert, Joyce, James, and Mallarmé, are valued not for their glacial transparency but for their density of sense and unlimited revelation.

VIII

In "El Aleph," Borges again travels the path of Desire through multiple incarnations of the object, the muse figure of Beatriz Viterbo, who constantly evades the word's embrace: "Beatriz Viterbo, de perfil, en colores; Beatriz, con antifaz, en los carnavales de 1921; la primera comunión de Beatriz; Beatriz, el día de su boda con Roberto Alessandri [etc.]" (A, 156). And again, as in "El Zahir," the writer escapes the frustration of everyday reality by entry into an ideal world, as embodied in the Aleph, "una pequeña esfera tornasolada, de casi intolerable fulgor" (169). However, in "El Aleph," Borges explores in greater depth the specular/cinematic ramifications of this strange device, which is structured on both the fullness of the imaginary and the emptiness of the symbolic.

---

[10] See Ong, 165-70.
[11] Cf. Alazraki (1971[ii]), 80, 84.

Within the context of his work, the artist rediscovers that paradoxical combination of closeness and distance, of the concrete and the abstract. Since language, as a *medium,* is by definition restricted to the mid-ground between these two extremes, it is fundamentally unable to express what the eyes have grasped as a totality. Hence the frustration of the Romantic:

> Arribo, ahora, al inefable centro de mi relato: empieza, aquí, mi desesperación de escritor. Todo lenguaje es un alfabeto de símbolos cuyo ejercicio presupone un pasado que los interlocutores comparten; ¿cómo transmitir a los otros el infinito Aleph, que mi temerosa memoria apenas abarca? [. . .] En ese instante gigantesco, he visto millones de actos deleitables o atroces; ninguno me asombró como el hecho de que todos ocuparan el mismo punto, sin superimposición y sin transparencia. Lo que vieron mis ojos fue simultáneo: lo que transcribiré, sucesivo, porque el lenguaje lo es. Algo, sin embargo, recogeré. (168-9)

Closeness is here conveyed by the sheer intimacy of the experience: the Aleph is a mirror in which the subject perceives not merely the whole world but himself ("vi mi cara" [171]). Distance, on the other hand, correlates with the disembodied gaze: voyeurism, like sadism, always keeps apart the *object* and the *source* of the drive; to fill the distance would be to overwhelm the subject.[12]

What the dichotomy of closeness/distance encapsulates is the idealistic mechanism whereby a subject is separated from the object. Only through productive work can we truly relate as subjects to the world of objects around us, that is to say, through creative praxis that makes us feel at home in the world, instead of alienating us from it. But since the idealist rests his case upon a division of labour which separates practice from theory, this sense of at-homeness is denied him. One consolation remains: to the extent that his "fictions" are anterior to things, the idealist can persuade himself that he is united with the object. Hence, finally, that oscillation between clean separation and total fusion that characterizes idealist texts.

If the writer must refuse the mystic vision on pain of incest – the specular image of his monstruous ugliness is the price that his occa-

---

[12] See Metz, 58-59.

sional failure in this respect exacts – it is to transfer the illusion of fullness to the work of art itself, or rather to its technical appendages. The equipment is a fetish or substitute for the penis, which, at the same time as it exhibits its fullness or technical potency, affirms an absence. "The apparatus is a prop, that disavows the lack and in doing so affirms it without wishing to" (Metz, 58-59). This paradox is definitive of the status of the connoisseur, who goes to the cinema for pleasure, to be carried away by f[r]iction, but also to appreciate just as much the machinery that is carrying him away. As Carlos explains:

> Ya sabes, el decúbito dorsal es indispensable. También lo son la oscuridad, la inmovilidad, cierta acomodación ocular. Te acuestas en el piso de baldosas y fijas los ojos en el decimonono escalón de la pertinente escalera. Me voy, bajo la trampa y te quedas solo. (167)

Like any fetishist, he is uncompromising. Each detail, each aspect of the ritual, has to be met with: "–La almohada es humildosa – explicó –, pero si la levanto un solo centímetro, no verás ni una pizca y te quedas corrido y avergonzado. Repantiga en el suelo ese corpachón y cuenta diecinueve escalones" (168). Necessarily, Borges meets these demands with the impatience one would expect from a normal person: "Cumplí con sus ridículos requisitos" (168).

(Post-)modernism is the literary form of fetishism *par excellence.* Within the carefully circumscribed domain of the Aleph, the semiotic dismantles the symbolic. As Kristeva explains (Kristeva [1984], 64-65), such a process is tantamount to shifting the thesis towards the semiotic *chora*. The artist establishes an object as a substitute for the symbolic under attack. After all, locked within the crazy auditorium, outside of society, he needs all the help that he can muster: the primal scene/screen upon which he gazes threatens to overwhelm him with its untold, unsayable revelations.

Following the performance, the spectator must cope with the shock of returning to the real world. "En ese instante concebí mi venganza" (171): the modernist writer becomes a killjoy by cold-bloodedly destroying Carlos' fiction. He knows, like any classicist, that to be blinded by the light is a precondition of the possibility of language. To speak, we must perforce sleep: "Felizmente, al cabo de unas noches de insomnio, me trabajó otra vez el olvido" (172).

To function socially, we must forget: "Nuestra mente es porosa para el olvido; yo mismo estoy falseando y perdiendo, bajo la trágica erosión de los años, los rasgos de Beatriz" (174).

IX

The idealistic Yahoo marks the point of maximum repression of the body: he is literally gelded, blinded (i.e., symbolically castrated), and his feet are cut off, "para que el mundo no lo distraiga de la sabiduría" (IB, 142). Through this violent act the body is sacrificed; through this sacrifice all semiotic violence is curtailed. Without the murder of the soma, all order is impossible, and without order, there can be no representation.

At the same time, of course, the total ejection of all substance coincides with the maxium return of the repressed: the pleasure aroused by elimination coincides with a resurgence of anality.[13] Through their behaviour, the Yahoos betray the origins of civilization, in man's backside: "Para llamarse, lo hacen arrojándose fango" (141). Rejection either delays language acquisition or prevents it altogether. Living like animals in the present, the Yahoos are incapable of abstraction (and thereby of getting lost). Their culture of Dung calls into question the very conventionalism which the existence of language presupposes: a house is a "tree," and the anthropologist's Bible and compass are objects that are gathered or "collected" from nature. Concomitantly, however, the semiotic fluidity that characterizes their language is pervaded by idealism ("Cada palabra monosílaba corresponde a una idea general" [147]), which suggests a capacity for abstraction scarcely compatible with their supposed primitiveness: "los Yahoos, pese a su barbarie, no son primitiva sino degenerada" (148). Contrary to appearances, they are latecomers who have lost, not failed to discover, the art of writing, evidence of which survives in the form of primitive inscriptions. The same is true of the immortal inhabitants of the city. For if the latter is a deposit of accumulated sublimation ("la resplandeciente Ciudad," "la nítida Ciudad" [A, 14, 15]), to reach it we must first journey through its bowels ("región de negros laberintos" [14]). Necessarily, therefore, the tortured architecture of its superstruc-

---

[13] See Kristeva (1984), 151-2.

ture inherits the symbolism originally attaching to the anal product. By the same token, its inhabitants are idealists – "determinaron vivir en el pensamiento, en la pura especulación [. . .] Absortos casi no percibían el mundo físico" (20) – but idealists who betray the price of the division of labour, which separates the thinker from the maker, in the unlived lines of their bodies. Capitalism is a living death, from which we need, periodically, to escape: "A veces, un estímulo extraordinario nos restituía al mundo físico" (22). Elemental rain, like the carnival day, marks a period when the reality-principle can be legitimately suspended.

More fundamentally, the idealist's retreat into the private sphere calls into question the transcendental subject upon which mentalism rests. A rigidified classicism gives way at its core, its subject now reduced to a dung-covered dog who lives in a cave: "pensé que acaso no había objetos para él, sino un vertiginoso y continuo juego de impresiones." It is replaced by a fluid Romanticism, in which anal drives totally overwhelm the thetic: "Pensé en un mundo sin memoria, sin tiempo; consideré la posibilidad de un lenguaje que ignorara los sustantivos, un lenguaje de verbos impersonales o de indeclinables epitetos" (18). While it reinstates the body, however, the Romantic legacy also rejects it, as a consequence of which it generates merely *ideas* about the bodily, social processes. Emptied of its heterogeneous contradiction, withdrawn from material continuity and social imbrication, it postulates an activity which can only be a simulacrum of the drives. The loss or weakening of the Oedipal chains sets the signifier adrift, but within the bounds of the symbolic. The idealist subject mimics within this bodiless realm those stages previous to the phallic stage, indeed, even the mirror stage.

The individual, washed clean of matter, is a soul, a nobody: "soy dios, soy héroe, soy filósofo, soy demonio, y soy el mundo, lo cual es una fatigosa manera de decir que no soy" (22). To be real is to be immortal, but to be immortal is never to have been born. It is a Platonic paradox which in late capitalism assumes extreme forms: the idealist retreats into literature, which promises a more authentic experience than that otherwise possible in a consumer society, but outside of society experiences a loss of life ("un hombre consumido y terroso, de ojos y barba gris, de rasgos singularmente vagos" [7]).

Eternally returning, entrapped within a boundless, empty space, the immortal knows no *mother* tongue. He seeks a phallic presence with which to fill a hole caused by the lack of matter. Within the confines of idealism, however, he is destined never finally to close in upon himself: the river of mortality faithfully reproduces the image of its antagonist, with all its shortcoming. This failure is predictable, even necessary, and of course profoundly political. Idealism must refuse a genuine dialectic, which can only be a species of dialectical materialism. And with this refusal the immortal "must remain ignorant not only of his functioning as social practice, but also of his chances for experiencing jouissance or being put to death" (Kristeva [1984], 142).

CONCLUSION

The triumph of liberalism in Argentina between 1850 and 1920 was attended by a radical division of labour which pitted the non-manual elements of society against the masses. Towards the end of the century, this division deepens for several reasons. Firstly, the more traditional fraction of the hegemonic class attempts to preserve such cherished values as the "freedom of the individual," a freedom increasingly at risk in the climate of monopoly capitalism. Secondly, the bourgeoisie also faced the ominous prospect of the rise of socialism and even the terrifying spectre of a proletarian revolution. As a result, not only does the writer retreat into his own private, literary world, but within this world reproduces that same division of labour which initially splits theory from practice:

> El pensativo, el hombre intelectual vive en la intimidad de los conceptos que son abstracción pura; el sensitivo, el carnal, en la contigüidad del mundo externo. Ambas trazas de gente pueden recabar en las letras levantada eminencia, pero por caminos desemejantes. El pensativo, al metaforizar, dilucidará el mundo externo mediante las ideas incorpóreas que para él son lo entrañal e inmediato; el sensual corporificará los conceptos. (I, 148-9)

One is struck less by the difference between these two character-types than by what, as mirror images, they share, namely a lack of any conception of the dialectical processes involved in the production of knowledge. In this respect, they both attest to the impact of a consumer society which marginalizes the whole notion of labour. In literary terms, this marginalization corresponds with the absence of any understanding of the production of texts. Borges' classicism, by emphasizing the transparency of language, conjures away the medial objectivity of the work. It combines with certain neo-idealist trends to transform the consumption of the text into a direct spiritual encounter between the souls of the writer and the reader. The critic intervenes, if at all, to facilitate the lovers' tryst, as a sort of go-between, quick to withdraw once all obstacles have been removed.

It is the illusion of all lovers that they come together on neutral ground, within a private space remote from all the pressures of history and social circumstance. But their discourse is anything but innocent of extra-textual implication. For while idealism may be said to be a permanent temptation to mankind, it always assumes localized, ideologically motivated forms. The social body that is rejected by the Argentinian bourgeoisie is that of the growing industrial proletariat of Buenos Aires. The hegemonic class simply dissolves the reality that threatens it, thereby denying the subject any dialectical contact with the object. Ceasing to love others, the subject regresses to self-love.

In the curious situation of Argentina, developments in the capitalist mode of production have been telescoped in such a manner that later stages are superimposed on pre-industrial stages. Just as the mechanically programmed, dehumanized, even fantasmal forms of the City of the Immortals and the closed, inexorable cycles of the agriculturally based community have come to share a common language in myth, so the sophisticated modernist like Borges claims to speak in the voice of an ancient tradition. In the light of such overdetermined cultural situations, Tzinacán, in "La escritura de Dios," assumes a certain archetypal status. Socially marginalized and historically vestigial, he is able, from his transcendental position, to range dispassionately across the totality, equally at home in all cultures or rather equally estranged from them all: "Vi infinitos procesos que formaban una sola felicidad y, entiéndolo todo, alcancé también a entender la escritura del tigre" (A, 123).

It is not this universalism alone that indicates the modernist's complicity with international capitalism. For in his concern for the preservation of the self, he presides over its dissolution, in a way singularly in keeping with the cold indifference of capitalist production towards the individual. While the neo-classical renaissance of the 1920s onwards re-affirms the thetic break, it is unable to stem totally the irruption of the drives into the symbolic, which accordingly enters into process. Indeed, it can be justly maintained that post-liberal capitalism is characterized by the gradual effacement of the distinction between the ego and the unconscious in a narcissistic personality type.[1] This explains the intuitive immediacy and intimacy of the contact between the writer and his work, and the aura of sensibility with which it is shrouded:

> Un hombre se propone la tarea de dibujar el mundo. A lo largo de los años puebla un espacio con imágenes de provincias, de reinos, de montañas, de bahías, de naves, de islas, de peces, de habitaciones, de instrumentos, de astros, de caballos y de personas. Poco antes de morir, descubre que ese paciente laberinto de líneas traza la imagen de su cara. (H, 155-6)

The contradictions within capitalism, we reiterate, can only be understood in their specificity. In Argentina the colonist, for centuries the victim of Spanish, British and more recently North American imperialism, has less the sense of transcendental omnipotence and omniscience than of emptiness and insubstantiality. The literary consequences are only too obvious in Borges: while it speaks to the condition of the colonizer, the autonomous, self-confident subject of realistic novels is irrelevant to that of the colonized, who finds more meaningful the fantasies of a faded subject.[2] Wherever we turn in Borges we discover the same ghostly subject striving to flesh itself out with a body that regressively eludes its grasp: "Sentí, en la última página, que mi narración era un símbolo del hombre que yo fui, mientras la escribía y que, para redactar esa narración, yo tuve que redactar esa narración, y así hasta lo infinito" (A, 104).

By a strange paradox, however, a peripheral writer such as Borges, who rejects the national mythology of Romanticism, finds himself suddenly elected as the perfect ideologue of a disembodied centre.[3] His credentials cannot be doubted: the self-imploding agents of capitalism correctly identify what is a familiar experience: "Volví a dormir; soñé que los granos de arena eran tres. Fueron, así, multiplicándose hasta colmar la cárcel y yo moría bajo ese hemisfe-

---

[1] See Dews, 230-2.
[2] Cf. Eagleton (1990), 321-5.
[3] Franco remains one of the few critics to have fully explained the paradoxical reversals of marginality and centrality in Borges, and the ideological appeal of his "free-floating adaptability" (Franco, 55, 78).

rio de arena. Comprendí que estaba soñando; con un vasto esfuerzo me desperté. El despertar fue inútil; la innumerable arena me sofocaba" (A, 121). In this way, the non-identity of the traditionalists chimes unexpectedly with the anonymity of the deracinated modernist.

The modernist isolation can be turned to advantage. His very solipsism is the means through which he will rekindle something of his former power. Withdrawn from a reality in which he is the passive, powerless victim of circumstance, he discovers a time when he was the whole universe and the monarch of all he surveyed. Needless to say, the maintenance through classicism of the thetic break indicates that post-modernism is far from succumbing to a hedonism of the flesh. The dissolution of the self's reflective unity can only mean, within its historical context, the triumph of a unifying process at a post-subjective level.[4] And if the resultant subject lacks all substance, so, we suspect, does the Aleph or the fourteen words that constitute for Tzinacán the key to the Absolute. It requires no particular acumen to discern in them the barely disguised form of the commodity: intimate yet desexualized, the latter contains within itself, as within one huge metaphor, the totality of signifiers which, in their abstraction and indeterminacy of value, can be freely exchanged, as in any good commercial transaction.

The political consequences are predictable. Critical distinctions, such as that between appearance and reality, are drawn by an active, fully-developed subject. The weak, narcissistic self is, by definition, precluded from any critical engagement with the real world: "Es dudoso que el mundo tenga sentido" (OI, 175). Necessarily, it succumbs to a proliferation of perspective that paralyses the will. This in turn induces a craven submissiveness to the political status quo, or alternatively to the arbitrariness of judgement which typifies the self-opinionated. Without presence, caught up in a constant play of difference, the subject is both everything and nothing, and Reason, both the ultimate answer and no answer at all: "Quien ha entrevisto el universo, quien ha entrevisto los ardientes designios del universo, no puede pensar en un hombre, en sus triviales dichas o desventuras, aunqe ese hombre sea él" (A, 123). One man's wisdom is another's cold-blooded cynicism.

---

[4] Cf. Tealdi, 25-26.

The refusal of an ultimate perspective finds expression artistically both in a fictional form which acknowledges its own illusory nature, and in a kind of discourse parasitic upon the very philosophical systems that it so subversively parodies. What the exponents of such perspectivism fail to perceive is that it is itself the effect of a capitalist totality that it pretends to evade. Furthermore, Borges misconstrues his solipsistic isolation as the "human condition," from whose lineaments he excludes, by implication, any genuine sense of social solidarity, other than the tradition of writers, his predecessors. Tragically, this tradition was the only community of which he appears to have conceived or indeed been aware.

BIBLIOGRAPHY

Adorno, Theodor W. and Max Horkheimer, *The Dialectic of Enlightenment*. Trans. John Cumming. New Hork: Herder and Herder, 1972.
Aizenberg, Edna. *The Aleph Weaver: Biblical, Kabbalistic Judaic Elements in Borges*. Potomac: Scripta Humanistica, 1984.
Alazraki, Jaime. "Oxymoronic Structure in Borges' Essays" (1971[i]). See Dunham and Ivask, 47-53.
———. "Kabbalistic Traits in Borges." *Studies in Short Fiction*. 8 (1971[ii]), 78-92.
———. *La prosa narrativa de Jorge Luis Borges: temas-estilo*. Madrid: Gredos, 1974.
Bakhtin, M. M. *Rabelais and His World*. Trans. Helene Iswolsky. Cambridge, Massachusetts/London: Massachusetts Institute of Technology Press, 1968.
———. *The Dialogic Imagination: Four Essays*. Ed. Michael Holoquist. Trans. Caryl Emerson and Michael Holquist. Austin, Texas: Texas U.P., 1981.
Balderston, Daniel. "Historical Situations in Borges." *Modern Language Notes*, 105 (1990), 331-50.
Barnatán, Marcos Ricardo. *Borges*. Madrid: E.P.E.S.A., 1972.
Barrenechea, Ana María. *Borges the Labyrinth Maker*. Ed. and trans. Robert Lima. New York: New York U.P., 1965.
Bell-Villada, Gene H. *Borges and His Fiction: A Guide to his Mind and Art*. Chapel Hill: North Carolina U.P., 1981.
Belsey, Catherine. *Critical Practice*. London/New York: Methuen, 1980.
Bennett, Tony. *Formalism and Marxism*. London/New York: Methuen, 1979.
Beverley, John. "The Production of Solitude: Góngora and the State." *Ideologies & Literature*. 3 (1980), 23-41.
Bickel, Gisele. "La alegoría del pensamiento." *Modern Language Notes*. 88 (1973), 295-316.
Blanco Aguinaga, Carlos, Julio Rodríguez Puértolas, Iris M. Zavala. *Historia social de la Literatura española (en lengua castellana)*. 3 vols. 2nd ed. Madrid: Castalia, 1986.
Blanco González, Manuel. *Jorge Luis Borges*. Mexico: De Andrea, 1963.
Bloch, Ernst, *et al*. *Aesthetics and Politics*. London: Verso, 1984.
Bloom, Harold. *The Anxiety of Influence: A Theory of Poetry*. New York: Oxford U.P., 1973.
———. *A Map of Misreading*. New York: Oxford U.P., 1975 (i).
———. *Kabbala and Criticism*. New York: Seabury Press, 1975 (ii).
Borges, Jorge Luis. *Inquisiciones*. Buenos Aires: Proa, 1925.
———. *El tamaño de mi esperanza*. Buenos Aires: Proa, 1926.
———. *El idioma de los argentinos*. Buenos Aires: M. Gleizer, 1928.
———. *Evaristo Carriego* (1930). Buenos Aires: Emecé, 1955.
———. *Discusión* (1932). Buenos Aires: Emecé, 1957.

Borges, Jorge Luis. *Historia de la eternidad* (1936). Buenos Aires: Emecé, 1953.
———. *Historia universal de la infamia* (1935). Buenos Aires: Emecé, 1954.
———. *Ficciones* (1944). Buenos Aires: Emecé, 1956. Madrid: Alianza, 1971.
———. *El Aleph* (1949). Buenos Aires: Emecé, 1957. Madrid: Alianza, 1971.
———. *Otras inquisiciones* (1952). Buenos Aires: Emecé, 1960.
———. *Obra poética.* Buenos Aires: Emecé, 1960. Madrid: Alianza, 1972.
———. *El hacedor.* Buenos Aires: Emecé, 1960. Madrid: Alianza, 1972.
———. *El informe de Brodie.* Buenos Aires: Emecé, 1970.
———. *El libro de arena.* Buenos Aires: Emecé, 1975.
———. *Prólogos con un prólogo de prólogos.* Buenos Aires: Torres Agüero, 1975.
———. *Siete noches.* Epilogue by Roy Bartholomew. Mexico/Madrid/Buenos Aires: Fondo de Cultura Económica, 1980.
——— and Adolfo Bioy Casares. *Crónicas de Busto Domecq.* Buenos Aires: Losada, 1967.
Brodzki, Bella. "'She was unable not to think': 'Emma Zunz' and the Female Subject." *Modern Language Notes,* 100 (1985), 33-47.
Bronowski, J. and Bruce Mazlish. *The Western Intellectual Tradition: From Leonardo to Hegel.* Harmondsworth: Penguin Books, 1963.
Brown, Norman O. *Love's Body.* New York: Vintage Books, 1966.
———. *Life against Death: The Psychoanalytical Meaning of History.* London: Sphere Books, 1968.
Burgin, Richard. *Conversations with Jorge Luis Borges.* New York/Chicago/San Francisco: Holt, Rinehart & Winston, 1968/69.
Caballero, Manuel. *Latin America and the Comintern: 1914-1943.* Cambridge: Cambridge U.P., 1986.
Christ, Ronald J. *The Narrow Act: Borges' Art of Allusion.* New York/London: London U.P., 1969.
Christmann, Hans Helmut. "Idealism," in Rebecca Posner and John N. Green (eds), *Trends in Romance Linguistics and Philology.* The Hague: Mouton, 1980. II, 259-83.
Cohen, J. M. *Jorge Luis Borges.* Edinburgh: Oliver & Boyd, 1973.
Correas, Gonzalo. *Trilingüe de tres artes de las tres lenguas castellana, latina, griega, todas en romance.* Salamanca: A. Ramírez, 1627.
Coward, Rosalind and John Ellis. *Language and Materialism: Developments in Semiology and the Theory of the Subject.* Boston/London/Henley: Routledge & Kegan Paul, 1977.
Croce, Benedetto. *Estetica come scienza dell'espressione e linguistica generale: teoria e storia.* 3rd ed. Bari: Gius Lateza & Figli, 1908.
Dews, Peter. *Logics of Disintegration: Post-Structuralist Thought and the Claims of Critical Theory.* London/New York: Verso, 1987.
Devonish, Hubert. *Language and Liberation: Creole Language Politics in the Caribbean.* London: Karia Press, 1986.
Dunham, Lowell and Ivor Ivask (eds). *The Cardinal Points of Borges.* Norma, Oklahoma U.P., 1971.
Eagleton, Terry. *Walter Benjamin or Towards a Revolutionary Criticism.* London/New York: Verso, 1981.
———. *The Function of Criticism: From "The Spectator" to Post-Structuralism* London: NLB, 1984.
———. *The Ideology of the Aesthetic.* Oxford/Cambridge: Basil Blackwell, 1990.
Echavarría, Arturo. *Lengua y literatura de Borges.* Barcelona: Ariel, 1983.
Ehrenzweig, Anton. *The Hidden Order of Art: A Study in the Psychology of Artistic Imagination.* London: Paladin, 1970.

Entwistle, William J. *The Spanish Language: Together with Portuguese, Catalan and Basque*. 2nd ed. London: Faber and Faber, 1962.
Fekete, John. *The Critical Twilight: Explorations in the Ideology of Anglo-American Literary Theory from Eliot to McLuhan*. London/Henley/Boston: Routledge & Kegan Paul, 1977 [1978].
Fernández Retamar, Roberto. *Caliban: Notes towards a Discussion of Culture in Our Latin America*. Trans. Lynn Garafola, David Arthur McMurry, Robert Márquez. Amherst: Massachusetts, 1974.
Ferrer, Manuel. *Borges y la Nada*. London: Tamesis, 1971.
Foster, David William. "Borges and Structuralism: Toward an Implied Poetics." *Modern Fiction Studies*. 19 (1973), 341-51.
Foucault, Michel. *The Order of Things: An Archaeology of the Human Sciences*. London: Tavistock, 1970.
———. *The History of Sexuality: Volume 1: An Introduction*. Trans. Robert Hurley. Harmondsworth: Penguin, 1981.
Franco, Jean. "The Utopia of a Tired Man." *Social Text*. 2 (1) (1981), 52-78.
Freud, Sigmund. *Case Histories II: "Rat Man," Schreber, "Wolf Man," Female Sexuality*. Vol. IX of the Pelican Freud Library. Trans. James Strachey, ed. Angela Richards. Harmondsworth: Penguin Books, 1979.
———. *On Psychopathology: Inhibitions, Symptoms and Anxiety and Other Works*. Vol. X of the Pelican Freud Library. Trans. James Strachey, ed. Angela Richards. Harmondsworth: Penguin Books, 1979.
———. *On Metapsychology: The Theory of Psychoanalysis*. Vol. XI of the Pelican Freud Library. Trans. James Strachey, ed Angela Richards. Harmondsworth: Penguin Books, 1984.
———. *Art and Literature*. Vol. XIV of the Pelican Freud Library. Trans. James Strachey, ed. Albert Dickson. Harmondsworth: Penguin Books, 1985.
Gertel, Zunilda. *Borges y su retorno a la poesía*. New York: University of Iowa and Las Americas, 1967.
Giovanni (eds), Norman Thomas di, Daniel Halpern, and Frank MacShane. *Borges on Writing*. London: Allen Lane, 1974.
Girard, René. *Violence and the Sacred*. Trans. Patrick Gregory. Baltimore/London: Johns Hopkins U.P., 1977.
Goldmann, Lucien. *The Hidden God: A Study of Tragic Vision in the "Pensées" of Pascal and the Tragedies of Racine*. Trans. Philip Thody. London: Routledge and Kegan Paul, 1964.
Gombrich, E. H. *Art and Illusion. A Study of the Psychology of Pictorial Representation*. 5th ed. Oxford: Phaidon Press, 1977.
Hall, Jr, R. A. *Idealism in Romance Linguistics*. Ithaca: Cornell U.P., 1963.
Hart, Jr, Thomas R. "The Literary Criticism of Jorge Luis Borges." *Modern Language Notes*. 78 (1963), 489-503.
Hegel, G. W. F. *Hegel: The Essential Writings*. Ed. and introd. by Frederick G. Weiss. New York: Harper & Row (Torchbooks), 1974.
How, Virginia K. "*Les Pensées*: Paradox and Signification." *Yale French Studies*. 49 (1973), 120-31.
Hughes, H. Stuart. *Consciousness and Society: The Reorientation of European Social Thought: 1890-1930*. St. Albans, Herts: Paladin, 1974.
Iordan, I. and J. Orr. *An Introduction to Romance Linguistics: Its Schools and Scholars*. Rev., with a supplement "Thirty Years On" by R. Posner. Oxford: Basil Blackwell, 1970.
Irby, James, Napoleon Murat, Carlos Peralta. *Encuentro con Borges*. Buenos Aires: Galerna, 1968.

Jameson, Fredric. *Marxism and Form: Twentieth-Century Dialectical Theories of Literature.* Princeton: Princeton U.P., 1971.
———. *Fables of Aggression: Wyndham Lewis, the Modernist as Fascist.* Berkeley/Los Angeles/London: California U.P., 1979.
———. *The Political Unconscious: Narrative as a Socially Symbolic Act.* Ithaca, New York: Cornell U.P., 1981.
Josipovici, Gabriel. *The World and the Book: A Study of Modern Fiction.* Frogmore, St Albans, Herts: Paladin, 1973.
Krieger, Murray. *The New Apologists for Poetry.* Minneapolis: Minnesota U.P., 1956.
Kristeva, Julia. *Desire in Language: A Semiotic Approach to Literature and Art.* Ed. Leon S. Roudiez. Trans. Thomas Gora, Alice Jardine, and Leon S. Roudiez. New York: Columbia U.P., 1980.
———. *Powers of Horror: An Essay on Abjection.* Trans. Leon S. Roudiez. New York: Columbia U.P., 1982.
———. *Revolution in Poetic Language.* Trans. Margaret Waller. Introd. Leon S. Roudiez. New York: Columbia U.P., 1984.
———. *The Kristeva Reader.* Ed. Toril Moi. Oxford: Basil Blackwell, 1986.
Lemaire, Anika. *Jacques Lacan.* Trans. David Macey. London/Boston/Henley: Routledge & Kegan Paul, 1977.
Lentricchia, Frank. *After the New Criticism.* Chicago: Chicago U.P., 1980.
Lichtheim, George. *Europe in the Twentieth Century.* London: Sphere Books (Cardinal), 1974.
Ludmer, Josefina. *El género gauchesco: un tratado sobre la patria.* Buenos Aires: Editorial Sudamericana, 1988.
Macherey, Pierre. *A Theory of Literary Production.* Trans. Geoffrey Wall. London: Kegan & Paul, 1978.
Manuel, Don Juan. *Libro de los enxiemplos del Conde Lucanor e de Patronio.* Ed. Alfonso I. Sotelo. 8th ed. Madrid: Cátedra, 1982.
Marx, Karl. *Grundrisse: Foundations of the Critique of Political Economy (Rough Draft).* Trans. with Foreword by Martin Nicolaus. Harmondsworth: Penguin Books, in association with New Left Review, 1973.
———. *Marx: Early Writings.* Trans. Rodney Livingston and Gregor Benton. Introd. Lucio Colletti. Harmondsworth: Penguin Books, in association with New Left Review, 1975.
Matamoro, Blas. *Jorge Luis Borges o el juego trascendente.* Preface by Juan José Sebreli. Buenos Aires: A. Peña Lillo. 1971.
Mazzeo, Joseph Anthony. *Renaissance and Revolution: The Remaking of European Thought.* London: Secker & Warburg, 1967.
Metz, Christian. *Psychoanalysis and Cinema: The Imaginary Signifier.* Trans. Celia Britton, Annwyl Williams, Ben Brewster, Alfred Guzzetti. London: MacMillan, 1983.
Molloy, Sylvia. *Las letras de Borges.* Buenos Aires: Sudamericana Sociedad Anónima, 1979.
Montgomery, Thomas. "Don Juan Manuel's Tale of Don Illán and its Revision by Jorge Luis Borges." *Hispania,* 47 (1964), 464-6.
Norman, Buford. "Thought and Language in Pascal." *Yale French Studies.* 49 (1973), 110-19.
Ong, Walter J. *Orality and Literacy: The Technologizing of the Word.* London/New York: Methuen, 1982.
Padley, G.A. *Grammatical Theory in Western Europe: 1500-1700: The Latin Tradition.* Cambridge: Cambridge U.P., 1976.
———. *Grammatical Theory in Western Europe: 1500-1700: Trends in Vernacular Grammar.* Cambridge: Cambridge U.P., 1985.

Passmore, John. *A Hundred Years of Philosophy.* Harmondsworth: Penguin Books, 1968.
Petras, James and Maurice Zeitlin (eds). *Latin America: Reform or Revolution?: A Reader.* New York: Fawcett Publications, 1968.
Petras, James. *Politics and Social Structure in Latin America.* New York/London: Monthly Review Press, 1970.
Pozuelo Yvancos, José María. "Norma, uso y autoridad en la teoría lingüística del siglo XVI." See Quilis and Niederehe, 77-94.
Prieto, Adolfo. *El discurso criollista en la formación de la Argentina moderna.* Buenos Aires: Editorial Sudamericana, 1988.
Pring-Mill, R.D.F. "Los calderonistas de habla inglesa y *La vida es sueño:* métodos del análisis temático estructural," in *Litterae Hispanae et Lusitanae.* Ed. Hans Flasche. Munich: Max Hueber, 369-413.
Quilis, Antonio and Hans J. Niederehe. *The History of Linguistics in Spain. (Studies in the History of the Language Sciences,* Vol. 34). Amsterdam/Philadelphia: John Benjamins, 1986.
Read, Malcolm K. *Juan Huarte de San Juan.* Boston: Twayne, 1981.
———. *The Birth and Death of Language: Spanish Literature and Linguistics: 1300-1700.* Madrid: José Porrúa Turanzas, 1983.
———. *Visions in Exile: The Body in Spanish Literature and Linguistics: 1500-1800.* Amsterdam/Philadelphia: John Benjamins, 1990.
Rodríguez, Juan Carlos. *Teoría e historia de la producción ideológica: I: Las primeras literaturas burguesas (siglo XVI).* Madrid: Akal, 1974.
Rodríguez Monegal, Emir. "Borges como crítico literario." *La palabra y el hombre.* 31 (1964), 411-16.
———. "In the Labyrinth." See Dunham and Ivask, 17-23.
———. *Jorge Luis Borges: A Literary Biography.* New York: E.P. Dutton, 1978.
Rodríguez-Puértolas, Julio. *Literatura, historia, alienación.* Barcelona: Labor, 1976.
Ruitenbeek, Hendrik M. *The Individual and the Crowd: A Study of Identity in America.* New York/Toronto/London: Mentor Books, 1964.
Running, Thorpe. *Borges' Ultraist Movement and its Poets.* Lathrup Village, Michigan: International Book Publishers, 1981.
Russell, Charles. *Poets, Prophets and Revolutionaries: The Literary Avant-Garde from Rimbaud through to Postmodernism.* Oxford/New York: Oxford U.P., 1985.
Sábato, Ernesto. *El escritor y sus fantasmas.* Barcelona/Caracas/Mexico: Seix Barral, 1979.
Shaw, D. L. *Borges: Ficciones.* London: Grant and Cutler in association with Tamesis, 1976.
———. Review of John Sturrock. *Bulletin of Hispanic Studies.* 55 (1978), 346-7.
Sorrentino, Fernando. *Siete conversaciones con Jorge Luis Borges.* Buenos Aires: Casa Pardo, 1973.
Sosnowski, Saúl. *Borges y la cabala: la búsqueda del verbo.* Buenos Aires: Hispanoamérica, 1976.
Stallybrass, Peter and Allon White. *The Politics and Poetics of Transgression.* London: Methuen, 1986.
Stead, C. K. *The New Poetics: Yeats to Eliot.* Rev. ed. Philadelphia: Pennsylvania U.P., 1987.
Sturrock, John. *Paper Tigers: The Ideal Fictions of Jorge Luis Borges.* Oxford: Clarendon Press, 1977.
Swietlicki, Catherine. *Spanish Christian Cabala: The Works of Luis de León, Santa Teresa de Jesús, and San Juan de la Cruz.* Columbia: Missouri U.P., 1986.
Tamayo, Marcial and Adolfo Ruiz-Díaz. *Borges, enigma y clave.* Buenos Aires: Nuestro Tiempo, 1955.

Tealdi, Juan Carlos. *Borges y Viñas: literatura e ideología.* Madrid: Orígenes, 1983.
Torres Villarroel, Diego de. *Vida, ascendencia, nacimiento, crianza, aventuras.* Ed. Dámaso Chicharro. Madrid: Cátedra, 1980.
Urrutia, Hernán. "Conocimiento, lenguaje y gramática en la obra de Andrés Bello (1781-1865)." See Quilis and Niederehe, 263-86.
Viñas, David. *Literatura argentina y realidad política.* Buenos Aires: Jorge Álvarez, 1964.
——. *Indios, ejército y frontera.* Mexico City: Siglo Veintiuno Editores, 1982.
Wheelock, Carter. *The Mythmaker: A Study of Motif and Symbol in the Short Stories of Jorge Luis Borges.* Austin/London: Texas U.P., 1969.
Williams, Raymond. *Marxism and Literature.* Oxford/New York: Oxford U.P., 1977.
——. *Politics and Letters: Interviews with New Left Review.* London: NLB, 1979.
——. *The Politics of Modernism: Against the New Conformists.* Ed. and intro. by Tony Pinkey. London/New York: Verso, 1989.
Wyers Weber, Frances. "Borges's Stories: Fiction and Philosophy." *Hispanic Review.* 36 (1968), 124-41.

NORTH CAROLINA STUDIES IN THE ROMANCE LANGUAGES AND LITERATURES

I.S.B.N. Prefix 0-8078-

Recent Titles

"LA QUERELLE DE LA ROSE": Letters and Documents, by Joseph L. Baird and John R. Kane. 1978. (No. 199). -9199-1.
TWO AGAINST TIME. A Study of the Very Present Worlds of Paul Claudel and Charles Péguy, by Joy Nachod Humes. 1978. (No. 200). -9200-9.
TECHNIQUES OF IRONY IN ANATOLE FRANCE. Essay on Les Sept Femmes de la Barbe-Bleue, by Diane Wolfe Levy. 1978. (No. 201). -9201-7.
THE PERIPHRASTIC FUTURES FORMED BY THE ROMANCE REFLEXES OF "VADO (AD)" PLUS INFINITIVE, by James Joseph Champion. 1978. (No. 202). -9202-5.
THE EVOLUTION OF THE LATIN /b/-/ṷ/ MERGER: A Quantitative and Comparative Analysis of the B-V Alternation in Latin inscriptions, by Joseph Louis Barbarino. 1978. (No. 203). -9203-3.
METAPHORIC NARRATION: THE STRUCTURE AND FUNCTION OF METAPHORS IN "A LA RECHERCHE DU TEMPS PERDU", by Inge Karalus Crosman. 1978. (No. 204). -9204-1.
LE VAIN SIECLE GUERPIR. A Literary Approach to Sainthood through Old French Hagiography of the Twelfth Century, by Phyllis Johnson and Brigitte Cazelles. 1979. (No. 205). -9205-X.
THE POETRY OF CHANGE: A STUDY OF THE SURREALIST WORKS OF BENJAMIN PÉRET, by Julia Field Costich. 1979. (No. 206). -9206-8.
NARRATIVE PERSPECTIVE IN THE POST-CIVIL WAR NOVELS OF FRANCISCO AYALA "MUERTES DE PERRO" AND "EL FONDO DEL VASO", by Maryellen Bieder. 1979. (No. 207). -9207-6.
RABELAIS: HOMO LOGOS, by Alice Fiola Berry. 1979. (No. 208). -9208-4.
"DUEÑAS" AND DONCELLAS": A STUDY OF THE DOÑA RODRÍGUEZ EPISODE IN "DON QUIJOTE", by Conchita Herdman Marianella. 1979. (No. 209). -9209-2.
PIERRE BOAISTUAU'S "HISTOIRES TRAGIQUES": A STUDY OF NARRATIVE FORM AND TRAGIC VISION, by Richard A. Carr. 1979. (No. 210). -9210-6.
REALITY AND EXPRESSION IN THE POETRY OF CARLOS PELLICER, by George Melnykovich. 1979. (No. 211). -9211-4.
MEDIEVAL MAN, HIS UNDERSTANDING OF HIMSELF, HIS SOCIETY, AND THE WORLD, by Urban T. Holmes, Jr. 1980. (No. 212). -9212-2.
MÉMOIRES SUR LA LIBRAIRIE ET SUR LA LIBERTÉ DE LA PRESSE, introduction and notes by Graham E. Rodmell. 1979. (No. 213). -9213-0.
THE FICTIONS OF THE SELF. THE EARLY WORKS OF MAURICE BARRES, by Gordon Shenton. 1979. (No. 214). -9214-9.
CECCO ANGIOLIERI. A STUDY, by Gifford P. Orwen. 1979. (No. 215). -9215-7.
THE INSTRUCTIONS OF SAINT LOUIS: A CRITICAL TEXT, by David O'Connell. 1979. (No. 216). -9216-5.
ARTFUL ELOQUENCE, JEAN LEMAIRE DE BELGES AND THE RHETORICAL TRADITION, by Michael F. O. Jenkins. 1980. (No. 217). -9217-3.
A CONCORDANCE TO MARIVAUX'S COMEDIES IN PROSE, edited by Donald C. Spinelli. 1979. (No. 218). 4 volumes, -9218-1 (set), -9219-X (v. 1), -9220-3 (v. 2); -9221-1 (v. 3); -9222-X (v. 4).
ABYSMAL GAMES IN THE NOVELS OF SAMUEL BECKETT, by Angela B. Moorjani. 1982. (No. 219). -9223-8.
GERMAIN NOUVEAU DIT HUMILIS: ÉTUDE BIOGRAPHIQUE, par Alexandre L. Amprimoz. 1983. (No. 220). -9224-6.

When ordering please cite the ISBN Prefix plus the last four digits for each title.

Send orders to: University of North Carolina Press
P.O. Box 2288
CB# 6215
Chapel Hill, NC 27515-2288
U.S.A.

NORTH CAROLINA STUDIES IN THE ROMANCE LANGUAGES AND LITERATURES

I.S.B.N. Prefix 0-8078-

Recent Titles

THE "VIE DE SAINT ALEXIS" IN THE TWELFTH AND THIRTEENTH CENTURIES: AN EDITION AND COMMENTARY, by Alison Goddard Elliot. 1983. (No. 221). *-9225-4.*
THE BROKEN ANGEL: MYTH AND METHOD IN VALÉRY, by Ursula Franklin. 1984. (No. 222). *-9226-2.*
READING VOLTAIRE'S CONTES: A SEMIOTICS OF PHILOSOPHICAL NARRATION, by Carol Sherman. 1985. (No. 223). *-9227-0.*
THE STATUS OF THE READING SUBJECT IN THE "LIBRO DE BUEN AMOR", by Marina Scordilis Brownlee. 1985. (No. 224). *-9228-9.*
MARTORELL'S TIRANT LO BLANCH: A PROGRAM FOR MILITARY AND SOCIAL REFORM IN FIFTEENTH-CENTURY CHRISTENDOM, by Edward T. Aylward. 1985. (No. 225). *-9229-7.*
NOVEL LIVES: THE FICTIONAL AUTOBIOGRAPHIES OF GUILLERMO CABRERA INFANTE AND MARIO VARGAS LLOSA, by Rosemary Geisdorfer Feal. 1986. (No. 226). *-9230-0.*
SOCIAL REALISM IN THE ARGENTINE NARRATIVE, by David William Foster. 1986. (No. 227). *-9231-9.*
HALF-TOLD TALES: DILEMMAS OF MEANING IN THREE FRENCH NOVELS, by Philip Stewart. 1987. (No. 228). *-9232-7.*
POLITIQUES DE L'ECRITURE BATAILLE/DERRIDA: le sens du sacré dans la pensée française du surréalisme à nos jours, par Jean-Michel Heimonet. 1987. (No. 229). *-9233-5.*
GOD, THE QUEST, THE HERO: THEMATIC STRUCTURES IN BECKETT'S FICTION, by Laura Barge. 1988. (No. 230). *-9235-1.*
THE NAME GAME. WRITING/FADING WRITER IN "DE DONDE SON LOS CANTANTES", by Oscar Montero. 1988. (No. 231). *-9236-X.*
GIL VICENTE AND THE DEVELOPMENT OF THE COMEDIA, by René Pedro Garay. 1988. (No. 232). *-9234-3.*
HACIA UNA POÉTICA DEL RELATO DIDÁCTICO: OCHO ESTUDIOS SOBRE "EL CONDE LUCANOR", por Aníbal A. Biglieri. 1989. (No. 233). *-9237-8.*
A POETICS OF ART CRITICISM: THE CASE OF BAUDELAIRE, by Timothy Raser. 1989. (No. 234). *-9238-6.*
UMA CONCORDÃNCIA DO ROMANCE "GRANDE SERTÃO: VEREDAS" DE JOÃO GUIMARÃES ROSA, by Myriam Ramsey and Paul Dixon. 1989. (No. 235). Microfiche, *-9239-4.*
CYCLOPEAN SONG: MELANCHOLY AND AESTHETICISM IN GÓNGORA S "FÁBULA DE POLIFEMO Y GALATEA", by Kathleen Hunt Dolan. 1990. (No. 236). *-9240-8.*
THE "SYNTHESIS" NOVEL IN LATIN AMERICA. A STUDY ON JOÃO GUIMARÃES ROSA'S "GRANDE SERTÃO: VEREDAS", by Eduardo de Faria Coutinho. 1991. (No. 237). *-9241-6.*
IMPERMANENT STRUCTURES. SEMIOTIC READINGS OF NELSON RODRIGUES' "VESTIDO DE NOIVA", "ÁLBUM DE FAMÍLIA", AND "ANJO NEGRO", by Fred M. Clark. 1991. (No. 238). *-9242-4.*
"EL ÁNGEL DEL HOGAR". GALDÓS AND THE IDEOLOGY OF DOMESTICITY IN SPAIN, by Bridget A. Aldaraca. 1991. (No. 239). *-9243-2.*
IN THE PRESENCE OF MYSTERY: MODERNIST FICTION AND THE OCCULT, by Howard M. Fraser. 1992. (No. 240). *-9244-0.*
JORGE LUIS BORGES AND HIS PREDECESSORS OR NOTES TOWARDS A MATERIALIST HISTORY OF LINGUISTIC IDEALISM, by Malcolm K. Read. 1993. (No. 242). *-9246-7.*
DISCOVERING THE COMIC IN "DON QUIXOTE", by Laura J. Gorfkle. 1993. (No. 243). *-9247-5.*

When ordering please cite the *ISBN Prefix* plus the last four digits for each title.

Send orders to: University of North Carolina Press
P.O. Box 2288
CB# 6215
Chapel Hill, NC 27515-2288
U.S.A.

The Department of Romance Studies Digital Arts and Collaboration Lab at the University of North Carolina at Chapel Hill is proud to support the digitization of the North Carolina Studies in the Romance Languages and Literatures series.

www.ingramcontent.com/pod-product-compliance
Lightning Source LLC
Chambersburg PA
CBHW030656230426
43665CB00011B/1127